MY BEST Service EVER

A Collection of Stories

*How organizations make a difference
and leave a lifelong memory through
the power of service*

**Mark Arnold
Rory Rowland
Quentin Templeton**

Copyright

Table of Contents

Acknowledgments

To Michaela, who has encouraged me to continue to reach for the stars. To Rory, under whose tutelage I have grown in ways I could never have imagined. To my familybecause their support for me in every venue of my life has enabled me to achieve greatness. Finally, to my mother, for her ability to always encounter the best service. ~ **Quentin Templeton**

~

Writing a book (even one with co-authors) is not something completed without considerable help from others. This book is no exception. Countless people, several of whom are listed below, assisted me.

I begin by thanking my wife, Michelle, to whom my portion of this book is dedicated. You continually inspire me to pursue and achieve my dreams. I could not have a more supporting and loving best friend. You make this journey of life meaningful. I also recognize my daughters Elizabeth and Hannah. Always know you girls mean more to me than any book, speech or job.

Thank you to Neighborhood Credit Union President/CEO, Chet Kimmell, who continues to teach me a great deal about executive leadership and vision.

Colleen Cormier, one of my valued colleagues, worked extensively on these stories as well. She strengthened the work at every phase, and I am grateful for her input and story collection. ~ **Mark Arnold**

~

To my wife Tedi, who has always given me the best advice ever. To my children Eliot, Josh, Michaela and JP who have taught me about life's best lessons.

In memory of my mother who taught me to be strong. To my father who taught me to dream. ~ **Rory Rowland**

Share with Me

I would love to hear from you! This book could not be completed without the help of hundreds of individuals who took the time to share the stories of the best service they ever received. I know that the next book will be even better, simply because you will add your story to it.

I invite you to tell me how this book has affected you and changed the way you think about leadership. Please tell me what you would like to see more or less of, and which story was your favorite. While you are at it, do not hesitate to tell me *your* best service story!

In addition to your best Service, I would like to hear about your best:

- Coach
- Teacher
- Salesperson
- Manager
- Meeting
- Soldier
- CEO

Or, any other idea you may have about the BEST you have received!

Write us and send your submissions to:

Rory Rowland
14401 Covington Rd.
Independence, MO 64055

Phone: 816-478-3249
Email: RoryRRowland@att.net

You can also submit a story or send an email by visiting my website at roryrowland.com.

21 Lessons of the Best Service

You will notice as you read the following lessons of service that each one is in an active tense. Service is action and the more you think in an action sense the more successful you will be. Service isn't passive. These are stories where service was delivered with passion.

1. **Go out of your way:** The best service providers go to extra lengths to provide what is needed, sometimes giving a little and sometimes giving a lot extra. These great providers of service helped create a customer that was loyal for life. These stories were remembered for a lifetime.

2. **Take responsibility:** Every story you read in this book has a common thread: personal responsibility. You absolutely cannot have great service without taking responsibility. This is not only for your actions, but also for the actions of your fellow employees. Even if your competitor makes a crucial mistake, by owning that decision, you have the amazing power to show that your business is better. You fixed it.

3. **Follow up:** Following up takes virtually no time, but the power and impact are timeless. Simply by sending that personalized thank you note or calling to make sure everything is going well, you can turn a mediocre sale into a powerful one!

4. **Personally tailor:** Service is all about making your product more available to more people. In an age of growing production, the way to stand out is to personally tailor your service to each individual. Get to know them. Remember their name. Learn about their family. These are all useful pieces of information that can help you show the customer their best options. Without this crucial data, you're shooting in the dark.

5. **Trust:** It's a key to relationships, so why isn't it a key to your service? If you don't trust your customers to make the correct decisions with your suggestions, why are you

even providing them? Trust them; they'll remember that you did.

6. **Become like family:** Read the stories in this book. After you have, come back to this lesson and think about its impact. How can you apply it? How can you become like family to each of your valuable customers? It starts with your first interaction and it never stops. Bringing them back isn't enough. You have to go farther. You have to push yourself harder.

7. **Fix mistakes:** One of the differences between good service and best service is fixing mistakes. Sometimes they aren't your fault. There are even occasions when they won't have anything to do with your business. However, by fixing them, you show customers that their problems are your problems.

8. **Set standards:** Your goal must be more than the best service that your customers measure your competition against, you must become the service they measure others against. Don't create best service one out of every one hundred times. Create best service as your standard and it will soon become your customers' standard.

9. **Relieve stress:** You customers are real people. They have problems, they have stress, and they even have bad days. One of your new goals should be to relieve some of those stresses in your customers' day. Above all, don't add to it!

10. **Fit budgets:** Sometimes your services are too expensive for everyone. Don't discredit the profit obtained by word of mouth and loyal customers. Being pleasant about affordability is what the best service stories are made of. You never hear a best story start with, "Well, I couldn't afford anything..."

11. **Never force a product:** Sales people who have limited skills sometimes attempt to force their product on the customer. Car sales persons can't even get away

from this horrible stigma. Don't start down that path! Be pleasant, be open, even explain all of your products, but never, ever push customers to buy something! Always remember to offer your services, if you don't ask, they may not take it.

12. **Protect:** Customers look to you to give them sound advice. Go beyond that. Keep their interests in your sights and protect them. If you save them money—even a dollar—you will have a customer for life.

13. **Make time irrelevant:** Best service stories often revolve around the topic of time. Far too often we place too much of an emphasis on closing times. If there are customers waiting, serve them. They took the time out of their day to come see you, why not do the same?

14. **Cater to their needs:** Great service goes beyond knowing the needs of customers. Go a step further and become the best. Cater your service to exactly what the customer wants and needs. Your ultimate goal is to create an individualized service that is perfect for each person. The results from this lesson alone are mind blowing!

15. **Become result-oriented:** Excuses are the lifeblood of good service. The best service is results driven and focused. The day that you stop blaming shortcomings on excuses and start focusing on results is the day that you head toward the best.

16. **Find unique, small differences to rise above your competition:** Don't reinvent the wheel. Find a small difference—a creature comfort—that you can provide that will propel you past your competition.

17. **Remember preferences:** Each of your customers is different. You have already taken the time to get to know each one of them. Don't forget that valuable information that got you where you are. Remember it and apply it when you see them again. Call them by name. Ask about their new baby. Each of these questions shows you care. Prove it.

18. **Have a personal stake in outcomes:** A personal stake in a positive outcome for the customer shows you are completely committed to seeing them get what they want. Don't just say you care, show it, prove it, and reap the benefits from it.

19. **Be easy and convenient:** In a time in our society when wants are fulfilled instantaneously, you have to be faster and more convenient than your competition. Being so will only bring in more customers.

20. **Become a backbone of support:** It is impossible to know what your customers are feeling as they walk in your door. A birthday, a funeral, a graduation, a sick child? Each of these affects people. Know what is wrong, and become that backbone of support people want. If you have the wonderful opportunity to provide more than your product, why pass it up?

21. **Eliminate job descriptions:** Customers don't know if you are the manager, the sales associate or the custodian. Their focus is placed on what they are looking for. Become a crucial part of their best service and offer to help, even if it's not in your job description. It is all right to not know the answer, but be the one to find out the answer.

22. **Create a feeling of belonging:** If you create a feeling of belonging, people not only want to come back, they want to bring others back with them. Make them feel at home, help them to relax, and enable them to succeed.

23. **Focus on wants:** Even if you can't provide exactly what they want, you have the power to find out who can. Don't send them away; send them to another place they are guaranteed to find what they are looking for. Good service is thinking your product can satisfy their wants. Best service is finding exactly what they want, even if you can't provide it for them.

24. **Listen:** Listening is just as powerful as speaking. We have two ears and only one mouth. Make sure you are using them in that proportion.

25. **Under promise and over deliver:** Make sure you always go the extra mile, for there it is never crowded. Although it's the 21 lessons of service, 25 are listed. Always go above and beyond!

After you have finished this book, go back and make a listing of your very own 21 Lessons of the Best Service. At the end, we have included space for you to do so. After you've made your list, rip out the page, copy it down, or place the book in a place you will see every day. Spend time each day to actively implement each of the lessons. You read the book, you discovered the strategies, now put them into practice and reap the rewards!

The Authors

Support When I Needed It Most
Anonymous

I believe that Southwest Airlines employs people who carry out their corporate ideals. This had a very powerful impact on my family two years ago.

July 27th of 2006, my life changed forever. My parents were traveling back from a weekend at the beach with my youngest child, Sidney, who was then five-years-old. They had taken her for a week of fun during the summer as a treat. Her older brother and sister were away at camp so this trip with the grandparents was greatly anticipated as a special time just for her.

On the return drive home, after a wonderful experience making sand castles, gathering seashells, and just being a family at the beach, there was a tragic car accident. My daughter was watching a movie in the back seat, my father was taking a nap in the passenger side, and my mother was driving. For a reason we will never know, my mother veered off the highway and struck a road sign sending the Ford Explorer into a severe roll.

My mother was killed on impact as the vehicle flipped toward her side first. The truck landed upside down. My father was severely injured in the accident, but managed to pull my daughter out before help could arrive.

My mother was an adamant user of car seats and I believe it is what saved my young child from a certain death. She was rushed by ambulance to a local hospital and then flown via life flight helicopter to Children's Hospital in Jackson, MS. Her injuries were extensive with multiple broken bones, deep cuts, and severe internal trauma. My father was immediately placed in intensive care with damages to his lungs and lower legs.

As the accident unfolded on a lonely highway in Eastern Mississippi, my father was able to call me. I work for a furniture manufacturer and was traveling with one of the company's sales representatives in Texas. My coworker immediately rushed me to the airport.

When we arrived at the Southwest ticket counter, I was allowed to access a gate agent right away. Within five minutes, she had me on a flight that was leaving for Houston within the hour. She put me on standby for a flight from Houston to Jackson, although it was oversold and only had 12 minutes between flights.

As soon as I walked on the plane, the flight attendants met my every need. They allowed me some extra time to catch my breath before the doors closed, helping me stay calm. When we got in the air, one attendant prayed with me while another worked on the phone with gate agents in Houston.

When I arrived in Houston, I was allowed to exit the plane first. I made it to the Jackson flight with a few minutes to spare. Somehow, the gate agents there cleared a bulkhead seat for me and had my boarding pass waiting as I ran up to the gate. I traveled from the tip of Southern Texas to Central Mississippi in less than three-and-a-half-hours. Amazing!

The baggage office arranged to deliver my luggage to a friend's home so that I could be rushed to the hospital without waiting. When Sidney was admitted to a room, flowers and balloons were waiting for her there, sent from the flight attendants at Southwest Airlines. One of the attendants even called me several days later to check on our situation and relay her commitment for urgent prayer.

I continue to be amazed at this organization. After things had settled down and I went back to work, my first flight was with Southwest two weeks later. When I checked in at the gate, the agent there, whom I had never met, remembered my name and asked how we were doing. It is wonderful to know that big business can still be people-focused, needs oriented, and individualized. As a result, I am a raving fan.

My daughter is healthy today, thankfully. I wish I knew who all the people were helping me on that hot day in June. Somehow, I would love to shake their hands and tell them in person how much I appreciate the acts of kindness not covered in any job description. Or, is it? What you do can impact lives in very powerful ways.

Rolled Out the Red Carpet
Carolyn Warden

"To give real service you must add something which cannot be bought or measured with money, and that is sincerity and integrity."
Douglas Adams

Hearing my brakes sound like they were going to fall off my car was especially frightening considering my situation. I was on business in Asheville, North Carolina—far from home—and had just had them worked on after a major car collision.

It was about 6:45 at night when they made their screaming noise, and I pulled into the first Honda dealership I found: Apple Tree Honda. As I pulled straight over to the service garage and began to gather my things, panic set in. I had a sales meeting the next day, needed to get there, and still had to continue my trip on to Knoxville the next day.

I was clearly upset as I walked over to the first person I found. Seeing my distress, he quickly responded, "Ma'am, why don't you sit down and tell me what you need." I explained the situation.

"Ma'am, I can tell you're upset, and although it is too late to have someone look at your car tonight, let me tell you what I can do. I'll give you one of our loaners, make a reservation at a hotel for you, and I'll have the first person at 7 a.m. take a look at the car for you. He asked for my insurance company information and my dealership's phone

15

number and told me that he would contact them for the payment, if it were accident related.

I was so incredibly grateful and told him that my first meeting was 10:30 a.m. He then told me about one of the local landmarks, the Biltmore Estate, gave me a map and even explained the highlights.

The next morning, after a wonderful night in a great hotel arranged by Apple Tree, I prepared for my presentation. I received a call at 7:00 a.m. from the car dealership telling me that my brakes needed a part to repair. He was ordering the part, and told me to keep the loaner as long as I was in town. I told him I would only be in town for the day, and we arranged for me to come over as soon as I was done with my presentation so I could get an update.

I needed to relax and I took him up on the offer to see the Biltmore Estate. The drive into the estate alone instantly calmed my nerves. After touring the mansion, I drove to my sales presentation, went back to the dealership, and learned that my car wouldn't be fixed until four that afternoon.

He asked if that would be a problem, and I replied that I just needed to use my time wisely since I still had a lot of work I needed to do.

He immediately walked me over to an empty office that had a phone and computer! I asked how I could get an outside line so that I could place my calls on my telephone credit card.

"Ma'am, don't worry about it. The dealership will pay for any phone calls you need to make."

Even after I explained that they were out of state and long distance, he insisted, "Ma'am, it is our pleasure. We're glad you stopped here, we'll take care of you."

I used his long distance while he took care of all my insurance paperwork so I wouldn't have to pay anything. I was even on the road by five! I got into Knoxville in plenty of time that night.

Even though Apple Tree Honda knew I would not be a repeat customer since I was from out of town, they rolled out the red carpet for not only his dealership, but also his whole town.

Even though this best service experience happened in 1988, I still vividly remember it and tell the story often during my sales presentations.

"I'll Take Care of It"
Michelle Seever

"Be alert to give service. What counts a great deal in life is what we do for others."

Anonymous

I was in line at the grocery store behind an elderly gentleman. He had one of those mechanical voice boxes that help him speak, but they can be a challenge to understand in a noisy area.

Immediately I felt a wave of compassion rush over me. He was obviously buying his groceries for the week and had a substantial number of items. The young man that was checking him out was probably 17 years old, if not younger. The transaction took longer than normal because it was difficult for the two of them communicate.

The total groceries probably came to $42 and some change. The elderly gentleman gave the checker a little over $30 and some change. The young man was trying to tell the elderly gentleman that he was about $12 short. The older man began to check every pocket, putting his hands all over his body to see if he could feel some extra cash. I would have gladly given him the money but I didn't want to embarrass him in front of a line of people.

The young man quickly told the gentleman, "Don't worry about it, it is taken care of." He then asked if the man would like to help to his car. The elderly

18

man shook his head, "Yes" and the young man helped him out to his car.

Someone else came to the checkout stand and it was then that I realized that the young man had paid the difference for the man, even though he was making just over minimum wage.

I was so inspired by his act of kindness that I told the manager what he had done. The manager said, "We will make sure corporate knows about this and make sure the young man is recognized for his 'I'll take care of it attitude.'"

A few weeks later, I return to the store and found myself once again in this young man's checkout line. I asked him if the store had recognized his kindness for helping that elderly man. He said, "How did you know about that"? I said I was in the store and I saw what he'd done and I was inspired by his actions.

The young man was obviously of humble origins and said, "Thank you. I appreciate you noticing," and then he went on as if it was no big deal. I still smile when I think of that store and what that young man had done.

So Great, I Want to Hire Her
Rueben Garcia

"Do what you do so well that they will want to see it again and bring their friends."

Walt Disney

For our 23rd wedding anniversary, my wife and I went to Logan's Steakhouse. I wanted to have an intimate dinner with just my wife, and our outstanding waitress provided just that!

She gave us all of the specials as she normally would, but once she discovered why we were eating there that night, her mood completely shifted. She asked us if we wanted Logan's to celebrate with us, or if we preferred a more private occasion.

Explaining that we would prefer a more private one, she adjusted her service accordingly. She would stand in the background and serve us quietly as we ate dinner together. It's hard to explain, but she found out how to take care of us the way we wanted to be taken care of.

After enjoying our great dinner together, I went over to the manager and explained how excellent our server was. He offered us coupons, and I told him I appreciated the gesture, but coupons would not be what would bring us back to Logan's Steakhouse—it would be our server that would bring us back.

I then told him how I worked at a financial institution, and if he didn't treat her right, I was going to come back and hire her! She was that good.

The Little Extra
Rory Rowland

"Every contact we have with a customer influences whether or not they'll come back. We have to be great every time or we'll lose them."

Kevin Stirtz

In my mind, great service is that "little extra."

In Custer, South Dakota, at Custer State Park, the front desk clerk, Wade, delivered on that "little extra."

I was in South Dakota for a strategic planning session for a client. As a part of the session, they had ordered flip charts to be delivered to the conference room. The plan was to put everyone's ideas up on the wall and decide which ones would be implemented.

In order to save time—and get through everything—I wanted to get all of the information recorded on the flip charts before the meeting started. However, when I walked into the room, the flip charts were nowhere to be found. It turned out that they were delivered extremely late and arrived just 15 minutes before the meeting was to start. In a last minute attempt to record everything, I planned to skip the buffet lunch that everyone else was enjoying.

When Wade walked into the conference room, I was feverishly scribbling on the charts to get them completed. He knew that the charts were late, and much more, he knew it was the hotel's fault. As he walked up to me, he leaned over and asked, "Did you get anything to eat, sir?"

Expecting the usual, "Sorry the charts were late," response, I didn't even look up from my scribbling as I muttered, "No, I need to get this done. But no problem, it has happened before." Which was completely true, this is not the first lunch I have had to skip because equipment was delivered late.

It was at that time that Wade touched my shoulder, causing me to look up at him. "How about I go get you a plate and bring it in here for you to enjoy? What would you like to drink?"

I was literally speechless. Wade understood. He got it. In fact, he went the little extra. Of course, the flip charts were delivered late, but I know that Wade cared about his clients, as apparent by his sense of duty.

The food was delicious and I conducted a wonderful planning session—on a full stomach, and I still remember how good that buffalo burger tasted. It was terrific, even if I did have to gulp it down. But, what made it remarkable is that he asked if there anything else he could do for me. That little extra made it one of the best service experiences I ever had.

You're a Guest of The Davenport
Nancy Pullen

"Excellence is not an accomplishment. It is a spirit, a never ending process."

Lawrence M. Miller

The best service story I ever heard was from The Davenport Hotel in Spokane, Washington. As a meeting planner, I have planned events at many hotels for thousands of people, but The Davenport always does a great job. A historic hotel in Spokane, Washington with wonderful architecture, The Davenport is adorned with a lobby that feels like a time capsule. If you are ever in Spokane, stay at the Davenport Hotel.

While holding a conference there, I mentioned to one of the many attentive employees that we had received great service at the hotel each time we had come. He then told me that The Davenport management team utilizes stories to help illustrate their level of service. He went on to tell me that a local elderly woman eating lunch is a common sight in the lobby.

The staff really came to know her, as she would frequently come in to eat her lunch and enjoy the beautiful sights of the lobby. One day, on one of her first visits, she walked in and opened her brown sack to enjoy her lunch in their terrific lobby. Seeing her sitting there, a new employee got her what the hotel business calls "a set up." He placed a glass of water on top of a tablecloth complete with a fork, knife, spoon and single flower in a small vase.

As he began to arrange the table for her, she started to protest. "You don't have to do this! I'm not a guest of the hotel. Young man, please, listen to me, you do not have to do this!"

After the young man finished he simply smiled at the woman and replied, "Welcome to The Davenport. When you're here, you're a guest of The Davenport."

Notes

1. In what ways do you show the devotion to selfless service as shown in the Southwest Airlines story?

_____

_____

_____

_____

_____

2. How will you implement 'the little extra?'

_____

_____

_____

_____

_____

3. Explain the never-ending process to excellence.

_____

_____

_____

_____

_____

Volunteered the Grill
Rory Rowland

Jenni Bryan, leader of the eastern Jackson County Missouri Down syndrome support group, yelled to her husband in the other room "Hey, Keith, we have over 50 people signed up for the Down Syndrome Guild picnic."

Keith walked into the kitchen, "That's a great turnout."

"But how will we feed them all?" Jenni responds, "We only have three grills."

Keith said, "Let's give Neil Beckman at Hy-Vee a call and see what he recommends." Keith called Neil, who works for Hy-Vee Grocery Store Chain and explained their dilemma.

Keith explained his dilemma to Neil, telling him that they were planning to use portable grills to cook the hamburgers for the picnic. Neil said that it would take forever to cook for all those folks using charcoal grills. "There is no way you can cook enough food for that many people on individual grills and get them fed on time."

Neil said, "I will go to the store, pick up the company grill and bring it to the picnic."

On the day of the picnic, Neil pulled in with a gigantic propane powered cooker that was chrome clean. It turned out that Neil took a day off from his job to stay and cook all the food for the families on Hy-Vee's grill. It didn't take any time at all to cook all the hot dogs and hamburgers on this super power grill. It was amazing to see someone representing his company volunteer to serve and support a group of families that were coming together because their children have Down syndrome.

As a father of JP, who has Down's syndrome it is comforting to know that there are people in the world who are willing to take their time to volunteer to help others who are less fortunate. But, this great act of service made our weekend a little brighter. Neil didn't want the accolades, but it is such a powerful example of great service.

Took the Extra Time
Quentin Templeton

"Here is a simple but powerful rule: always give people more than what they expect to get."

Nelson Boswell

For whatever ridiculous reason, I decided to take a statistics class online through my university. My professor was using software by NeXT Computers, Inc. After studying for an hour or two, I would get onto the site to take a test. When I would click on the links, a blank page would pop up.

After emailing my professor and explaining my dilemma, I received a response back stating that he fixed the problem and could access the test when trying it on his own computer. I studied again and got ready to take my first test. I clicked on the link, only to discover the same problem, a blank page.

Since the university didn't primarily use NeXT software anymore, I had to contact the company directly. I contacted their customer service department, where I left my cell phone number and awaited their call.

I was contacted an hour or two later by a friendly young man by the name of Curtis. I explained my situation to Curtis, who explained that there was an update sent out and my professor failed to update his tests. He could pull the data on his own computer since that's where the information was

29

stored, but it wasn't uploaded to the server, so no other computer could access the tests, thus the reason for the blank links.

I explained to Curtis that I had already contacted my professor and he didn't seem to understand what he needed to do to fix the problem. Curtis went that extra step when he asked for the campus technology's phone number.

He then connected us on a three way phone call and allowed me to sit in on the conversation as he politely explained the situation to the technology department and described to them what they needed my professor to do in order for his students to access their tests.

After hanging up with the campus, Curtis explained to me that if it didn't work in a day or two to call his personal extension and he would contact the professor directly. I thanked him profusely and expressed my gratitude in his ability to go over the top with his service. It was outstanding service! Moreover, the problem was fixed.

Extreme Trust

Anonymous

"Give trust and you'll get it double in return."

Kees Kamies

Like most people, I'm a sucker for impulse buying. I saw an advertisement for a complete bedroom set from Costco. I jumped in my Jeep Cherokee and drove the 20 minutes to my local Costco.

When I got there, I could only find the floor model of what I wanted. I saw the closest employee and explained my dilemma to him. He told me that they had three in stock, but they were literally flying off the shelves and that's why there weren't any for me to see. I asked for one, he told me to pull around the back, and he would help me load it up.

As I pulled my not so spacious vehicle up to the loading dock, I began to believe that there was no possible way that the things were going to all fit. When we started trying to load it all in, I knew there was no way. He ended up trying to help me shove the items into my car in such a way that I would still have room to drive and see my mirrors. After ten minutes of frustration, he said, "You know, this is crazy. Why don't you just take my truck?"

I was stunned. Was he joking? Does he know how far away I live? "What are you going to do," he asked, "Steal it? Just take my truck, bring it back, and you can take it all home at the same time."

I took him up on his gracious offer, loaded up my purchases (with room to spare) and away I drove. It was very impressive, if not a little bit extreme service. Nevertheless, it did help me out in a time of need.

A Guest
John Berra

"For us, our most important stakeholder is not our stockholders, it is our customers. We're in business to serve the needs and desires of our core customer base."

John Mackey

My wife and I were looking for some new patio furniture. We had searched around multiple stores and settled on a set at our local Target. Only when we went to buy them, they were out of stock!

The employee who helped us called three or four stores and found a location that had all of the pieces we wanted. It was about a fifteen-minute drive from our home.

When we arrived, not only did they have all of the pieces, but they also took the time to help us load them all, thanked us for driving further to get them, and apologized again for not having everything at the original store.

From the start of the transaction to the very end, each store did a great job making me feel like a true guest of Target!

My Corner Service
Teresa Mann

"Give the public everything you can give them, keep the place as clean as you can keep it, keep it friendly."
Walt Disney

My best service comes from the Washington, DC metropolitan area's Harris Teeter. They must have an initiative to make the customers feel like they're at the corner grocery store.

As soon as you walk in, you immediately hear, "Hello, how are you? Can I help you find anything?"

When you check out, it's like a flashback to the 1960s. "Did you find everything you need? Can I get your child a balloon? Can I help you get your groceries to your car?" I feel as though they are living in the past's great service industry.

I believe that it's a fantastic goal to have a company philosophy so ingrained in your employees that customers feel that corner grocery store friendliness.

Notes

1.) What "little extras" were described in each story?

_____

_____

_____

_____

_____

2.) How do you make customers feel like a guest?

_____

_____

_____

_____

_____

3.) Of the last three stories, which one is your favorite and why? What would you like to copy from these stories?

_____

_____

_____

_____

_____

Knew Our Wants
Anonymous

Celebrating our 35th anniversary, my husband and I did some research and decided that we would go to the J.W. Marriott Hotel in North Phoenix.

The pictures did not do it justice. The Marriott in North Phoenix is a beautiful hotel overlooked by mountains, and with a great golf course. After arriving, my husband and I decided to walk around the grounds before checking in. As we were trying to take in all the beautiful scenery, a woman walked by and asked, "Can I help you?" I explained that we were about to check in. Instead of the usual employee "not my job, I'm going to point you to the desk and walk off," Cristina stopped and began to talk with us. She asked what brought us to Phoenix and I explained that it was our 35th wedding anniversary.

She immediately walked us over to the busy front desk and started, I thought, to get us our room keys. All of a sudden, my husband and I are in a complimentary suite. After we went to dinner we returned to our fabulous suite to find cake, champagne, flowers and a card signed by the entire hotel staff. We never forgot her, or the Marriott, and we will go back every time. She listened closely enough to surprise us on our anniversary. That made it the best service I have ever had.

Tuned Her Ears to Our Requests
Elise Jones

"If we don't take care of our customers someone else will."
Unknown

We had just gone to see an amazing concert in Chicago and went to a diner to have a drink and bite to eat before crashing back at the hotel. We were all tired and hungry when we walked into the busy restaurant.

It took us forever to get a seat, but when we did, we quickly ordered our drinks and food at the same time. When I realized that I had forgotten to order my drink, I asked for a soda as the waiter was walking away. He kept walking and didn't even make a sign that he had heard me. When our food came, of course, I still didn't have a drink.

After our waiter walked away again, I had accepted the fate that it was just too loud and he didn't hear me order it. It was at that very moment that another waitress walked by and set a coke down in front of me. I turned around to see a smiling face reply, "I overheard you ask for a Coke and I think he couldn't hear. Enjoy!"

And, with that, poof, she was gone.

That waitress, whose name I will never know, made an impact on me. It's not the volume of the voice; it's the intent of your ears.

Sometimes it's the Recovery
Anonymous

"Do what you say you are going to do, when you say you are going to do it, in the way you said you were going to do it."

Larry Winget

It was a Saturday night and I was in charge of dinner. Like most self-respecting guys, I called the closest restaurant, an Outback Steakhouse, and ordered what we wanted and went to pick it up. When I got out to the car, I checked the bag to make sure that everything was there. Sure enough, it was missing items. We had wanted sweet potatoes instead of fries and I wanted an extra sweet potato.

I walked back in to tell the girl who helped me. She explained how sorry she was for the order being messed up and came back with another bag containing the sweet potato. I drove home, only to realize that someone had forgotten that I had ordered that extra sweet potato. That little extra sweet potato was forgotten.

I was somewhat frustrated at this point, not because I needed the potato, but because I didn't want to have to pay for something that I didn't get. So, I called them on the phone and the same girl who helped me before answered the phone. I asked, "I can live without the item, but is there some way that you can give me store credit or credit my account?" She again apologized profusely and then blew me away by putting me on hold...to go get the manager!

The first thing out of the manager's mouth is, "Sir, where do you live?" I was a bit take aback by the question, but told him anyway. He then tells me that the potato will be there in less than five minutes.

Three minutes later, a man pulls up in a truck, carrying my sweet potato and a note from the manager and the girl who helped me – again apologizing!

I thought, in this day and age—a time where we have to check the bag before pulling away from a restaurant—this was above and beyond great service. That's what I think great service is. It's going beyond and exceeding a customer's expectations. The recovery is sometimes more important than the delivery.

Treated Us like Royalty
Mike Sams

"He profits most who serves best."
Arthur F. Sheldon

For our 40th wedding anniversary, I set up a trip to The Homestead in western Virginia. I made all of the prearrangements and paid ahead of time.

As we pulled up their elegant drive, two gentlemen opened the doors to our car and welcomed us to The Homestead. Our car was driven off and we never saw it until we were ready to leave and our bags were already loaded for us.

I, mainly due to my inability to pay for a larger room, had paid for the smallest room possible. When we were directed to our room, it was the largest suite I'd seen in my life. As we stepped into it, the lights were on, music was softly playing, my suit was hanging up and our bags were already unzipped and ready for us.

For dinner, we were advised to go to the hotel's restaurant. We got there and three people greeted us, wished us a happy anniversary, and told us that our table was ready. After being escorted by all of them, they informed us that they would all three be our servers. I was stunned. "All three?" "Yes sir, we'll be your servers tonight."

It was almost embarrassing because they practically fed us. They would change our forks and even jump at the chance to catch our drinks a sip or two down from full. I'm the kind of guy that drinks a lot of water while I eat. As soon as I would set my drink down, they were there to fill it back up again.

They must have brushed the crumbs off the table a hundred times that night, keeping the table meticulous. When dessert time came, I figured being in Virginia, we should have cherries jubilee. The older of the three waiters brought it out and prepared it right there in front of us.

The next day we were scheduled to enjoy a lunch by the pool before checking out. As we sat down at the pool, a young man walked up and offered to clean our sunglasses. I was somewhat shocked. Never before in my life has someone offered to clean my sunglasses.

When we called the concierge to check out, we were told to relax in our room. Not two minutes later, the room was descended upon by two bellhops and the concierge himself. In the time it took for us to walk down to the entrance, our car was waiting.

The bellhops had already packed our bags and the car was shining after having just been hand washed. They really did treat us like royalty.

Treated Me like A Friend
Aaron Quintanilla

"Friendly makes sales - and friendly generates repeat business."

Jeffrey Gitomer

My best service story comes from Apple Computers. I have a new iPhone and love it dearly. Apple came out with a new upgrade that was supposed to fix a bunch of problems that I didn't have in the first place. However, in order to download new applications, I had to have the upgrade, so I went ahead of downloaded it. As soon as I did, I started to experience the exact problems it was supposed to fix. My battery life became noticeably shorter, and I started to drop all my calls.

So I did what anyone would do, I called Apple.

I called at 4:30 or so in the afternoon. The customer service representative actually sat and chatted with me as my phone was restarting. I felt very comfortable talking with him, and even felt like I could hang out with him. It's certainly not something that other companies do.

Usually you're put on hold while your phone is restarting and the customer service representative helps someone else and then comes back when he think that your phone has restarted. Not with Apple. He actually waited and wanted to make sure that my problem was fixed before he moved on to someone else.

Being so close to closing time, I asked him during our conversation when the service line actually stops taking calls. He told me that officially, the lines close at 5:00 p.m. However, he told me that representatives would stay until every call in their system is answered and the problems are fixed. He even told me that just last week someone had stayed until 9:00 p.m. to make sure that someone's birthday gift would work for them.

That dedication to completion of tasks really makes Apple's service the best service I've ever had. I feel that anyone who's willing to wait—even until 9:00 p.m.—to fix a problem is worth all of my business.

Notes

1.) How do you listen for voices not heard?

_____

_____

_____

_____

2.) When stepping foot in your store, are customers royalty? Can you make someone feel like royalty?

_____

_____

_____

_____

3.) How is your recovery? Do you have plans in case you need to recover?

_____

_____

_____

_____

Even In a Downpour
Anonymous

"Business is not just doing deals; business is having great products, doing great engineering, and providing tremendous service to customers."

Ross Perot

I was making probably the most daunting decision of my life, a new car. Over the weekend, I visited several car lots. On Monday morning, I called the one I was interested in and asked a few questions. They gave me all the details I wanted. He then rather surprised me by asking for my location.

I told him I was at work, half an hour away, and wouldn't be able to make it until Friday afternoon. He told me it would be no problem; he would just bring the car over for me! Half an hour later, he was outside my office with one of the cars I mentioned. I looked it over and decided that I didn't like the color. He drove off, brought me back a different color, and asked, "What about this one?"

I fell in love with it! Next thing I know he's outside emptying out my car and vacuuming it for me in the pouring down rain. He changed the plates and brought all the paperwork into my office for me to sign. I never had to leave my office, go into the rain, or even clean out my car. He took care of it all and completely blew me away. It was a nice touch.

Notarized in the Rain
Pat Holle

Along with my siblings, we wanted to sell our family farm and needed to get a few documents notarized. My husband and I went to our local bank, but were turned away because the paperwork wasn't the bank's documents. I was devastated as we had a limited amount of time to get the documents signed .

So here we are, wandering around downtown Annapolis, Maryland trying to find a place to notarize our document, all during a sudden torrential downpour.

When we were looking around for a notary at another branch of our bank, we happened to walk past a competing bank. Drenched and feeling like we had nothing to lose, we decided to try the competitor. They were happy to notarize our paperwork at no charge , even though we were not customers. I thought that was cool.

With all the paperwork done, we could sell the family farm, and get that load off our backs. A few weeks later we needed a certificate of deposit for the proceeds of the sale and I decided to open it with this branch.

I'd forgotten the employee's last name and guessed at her first name. When I mentioned my name and said I wasn't sure if she remembered me, she said, "You and your husband came to see me in the rain." She then opened a CD for us and it has distinguished them from all the other banks that day. Just for providing us with notary services, they stood out to us, and got all the proceeds from our sale invested with them in return.

Service to the Unknown
Anonymous

"Be the change you're trying to create."
Mahatma Ghandi

Some of the best service is the service you give to the unknown. My son experienced this very feeling one bitterly cold day while at college.

As he was walking home from a friend's house he saw a car with flat tire. He continued on home, got into his truck with his tire repair kit, and went to go fix the tire. He jacked the truck up, took the tire off, and repaired the leak.

The next day he was sitting in his humanities class and a young lady told the class that someone really restored her faith in people.

She went on to explain that she had called her boyfriend the night before explaining that she had a flat tire. Not knowing how to even get the tire off, they were both fearful of starting the daunting task. Let alone knowing where the money to pay for a replacement was going to come from. As they walked outside, they both saw that the once flat tire had been repaired and patched.

My son, sitting in the class, didn't know who she was or even who he was helping. But he did say that it was one of the most rewarding experiences in his life. It affected him on a personal level—his service to the unknown.

Ran To the Grocery Store For Me
Jennifer Cook

"If you work just for money, you'll never make it, but if you love what you're doing and you always put the customer first, success will be yours."

Ray Kroc

Unfortunately, my favorite service story comes from a restaurant that has since burned down: KT Fryer's. My family and I went for my birthday and I had looked forward to their thick and juicy southern fried pork chops all week long. When we got there, I was informed by our waitress that they had run out for the night.

Slightly devastated, I ordered something else. As soon as our waitress walked away, the owner walked up and replied, "You seem like you really want these pork chops." I told him I was, but completely understood that since they were so good, everybody must have wanted them. Before walking away, he asked, "Can you wait 20 or 30 minutes, and I'll see what I can do for you?" Mystified as to his plan, I agreed to wait.

It turns out that he went to the local grocery store and bought me the pork chop, prepared them, and hand delivered them. He didn't even charge me extra! It was 8:00 at night and he took the trouble to go to the grocery store and get some that were even the same quality as he usually serves.

Usually when a restaurant runs out of something, you think, "Why can't you just go to the grocery store across the street?" And this guy actually did. I'm sure he paid more than he would from his butcher, but it showed how much he cared about his customers!

Better than the Competition
Anonymous

"Although your customers won't love you if you give bad service your competitors will."
Kate Zabriskie

At a business conference at a Marriott hotel during one of the breaks, I really wanted a cup of tea. One of the staff saw me standing there staring at the provided options and walked up to ask if they could assist me.

I told him I'd really like a glass of tea. He explained that the conference didn't order tea, but he said if you wait just one moment I will get you some tea. Before I could stop him, he took off. A minute later he came back carrying a cup on a plate, hot water, and a little box with a variety of different choices of flavored tea. It was setting the bar higher than their competition.

Notes

1.) In a service aspect, how are you better than your competition?

_____

_____

_____

_____

_____

2.) How can customers tell that you love what you do?

_____

_____

_____

_____

_____

3.) How will you serve the unknown today?

_____

_____

_____

_____

_____

Made My Life Easier
Terra Ackeron

*"As far as customers are concerned you are the company.
This is not a burden, but the core of your job. You hold in
your hands the power to keep customers coming back –
perhaps even to make or break the company."*
Unknown

I was probably the happiest girl in the world. I
was getting married! When I called my local bridal
shop, Solution's Bridal, I was greeted by a friendly
voice that made an appointment with me.

They asked who would accompany me, and I
replied my mother and father. When we arrived,
there were seats for my parents. There was even a
newspaper sitting on one of the chairs for my
father! They made sure everything went smoothly,
even during the long process of dress shopping.

After my wedding, I received a call from them
asking to make sure that everything went off
without a hitch. They even asked me for pictures
to display in their shop! I was amazed at their
friendliness and they became my best friend.

Because of their willingness to go above and
beyond, I refer everyone that I know to Solution's
Bridal.

Worked To Fit Into My Budget
Danielle Easton

*"Customers today want the very most and the very best for
the very least amount of money, and on the best terms. Only
the individuals and companies that provide absolutely
excellent products and services at absolutely excellent prices
will survive."*

Brian Tracy

I was the chairman of the closing ceremonies
committee. With a dinner and entertainment for
1,500 on our plate, we scoured St. Louis to find a
location that would hold us and provide the
necessary requirements.

That search ended—we thought—the day we set
foot in The Science Center. It was certainly big
enough, and offered us the opportunity to use the
Imax theater to show two different movies, the
illuminated planetarium to hold our dance, and
even had the tables to hold our gigantic dinner
buffet.

Jessica, The Science Center's event planner,
walked us through the facility and explained each
feature and its associated cost. We were sold, that
is, until we got to the meal portion. It turns out
that the Center's contract caterer was Wolfgang
Puck's restaurant. As she showed us a menu, I
about died. The prices were around $20 per
person; something we certainly wouldn't be able to
afford.

As we watched the idea of us hosting at The Science Center melting from our grasp, she asked if the catering price was our only deterrent. The overwhelming opinion was yes. Other than that, the place was perfect!

She explained that she would talk to her boss and see what kind of deal they might be able to work out. For the next four days, my committee and I searched endlessly for a venue that was even half as good. We came up with a few choices, but everything paled in comparison to The Science Center.

I received a call later that day from Jessica who told me how excited her boss was to have us. He searched through policy and found an outside caterer that they had a contract through: Aramark Food Service. Although they very rarely used them, they were on the books, and so were we!

With prices nearly half, we reserved our spots and started planning for our event. But Jessica's great service didn't stop there. She gave me her personal cell phone number in case I needed something and her email address. She would even give me a courtesy call to tell me when she was about to email me something. Jessica and all of the Science Center's staff went beyond to make sure that our convention was the best ever! Especially true of this was their ability to fit not only our size, but also our budget. Something few other sites were willing to do.

Protected Our Assets
Elise Jones

I was enjoying a fun night out with a bunch of friends at a local Applebee's. My best friend Catherine was sitting next to me. As our waitress, Amanda, brought out our drinks, Catherine knocked over her full glass of water. With the whole table in jeopardy of being drowned, Amanda took a diving leap, screaming, "Oh my gosh, PHONE!" With that, she saved my brand new cell phone from being washed away in a flood of lemon-flavored water.

She immediately handed the phone to me and apologized for making the leap, but explained her worry of the phone being carried off by the imminent typhoon. She then instantly turned her attention to the table and asked if anyone needed a towel.

We had just received our appetizer and Amanda checked to make sure that none of the water got on any of us.

Her amazing service wasn't in her ridiculous dive over our sopping wet table, or her talkative style that made a possibly uncomfortable situation fine, but in her willingness to go beyond to make sure that an accident was taken care of immediately. Even though the ruined food wasn't her problem, she was more than willing to own it and bring out new food for us.

Became My Benchmark
Janine McBee

"There are no traffic jams along the extra mile."
Roger Staubach

Sometimes it's the simple things that make all the difference—like milk and cookies!

We were in the middle of a conference at the San Antonio Marriott River Center. At the end of Friday's sessions, I was talking with one of our hotel representatives, Roy Nieto. Through the years, he had become a special friend. We always caught up with each other about families when we saw each other.

That night, I mentioned that I was looking forward to my husband and young son joining me for the weekend. However, due to stormy weather, they were delayed. It was sounding like it might be midnight before they arrived.

To my surprise, later that evening, milk and cookies were delivered to our room. When my husband and son finally arrived, the surprise and delight in my son's eyes that milk and cookies had been sent for him was fun to watch.

That simple gesture is still fondly remembered today. The hotel remains one of my favorites, serving as a benchmark for what I have come to expect when it comes to service.

Flattered Me
Anonymous

"Customer satisfaction is worthless. Customer loyalty is priceless."

Jeffrey Gitomer

There is only one place I will buy my jeans. In Seattle, there is a GAP store in Broadway Market. As soon as you walk in, you're waited on hand and foot! There is someone there asking what you are looking for and you are directed to the appropriate department where there is an employee who specializes in that area.

When buying jeans, they always ask for your size and then they go find the jeans for you. When I tell them I'm a four, I always get the, "Oh no Honey, you look more like a 2, maybe even a 0."

It's just a very flattering experience. You're told how amazing you look and they encourage you so much. No matter who is working that day, it's just always a very great experience.

Notes

1.) What systems are in place to your customers' lives easier?

_____

_____

_____

_____

_____

2.) Do you set your customers' benchmark?

_____

_____

_____

_____

_____

3.) Do you continually build customer loyalty?

_____

_____

_____

_____

_____

A Guided Tour
Mike Inkenbrook

"Always do more than is required of you."
George S. Patton

I've stayed at many different hotels in my years of travel. However, the best experience I've had came from possibly one of the smallest hotels I've stayed at.

The Hyatt Place in Topeka, Kansas is not a big hotel by any means. As soon as I checked in, the agent behind the counter took me around the hotel lobby. He showed me where I could buy a drink and how to have it put on my room bill, where we get breakfast, the bar, and where the business room was. I could even print anything out from my room and have it held at the front desk for me!

He then walked me over to the elevator and told me what floor I was on, and even gave me directions for when I got off the elevator to get to my room! It was a very nice tour as I walking in, especially for a relatively small hotel. It was a very nice touch.

Never Pushes Products on Me
Kay Murray

*"Forget about the sales you hope to make and concentrate
on the service you want to render."*
Harry Bullis

I've always been an Acura girl. There is just
something about that sporty, sun in your eyes kind
of car that appeals to me. That was, until I decided
to try a Lexus.

I first had a Lexus 330. Quite a jump from my
sporty Acura predecessors! After four months, I
turned the car back into the dealership. While
signing all the paperwork, my dealer asked why I
was changing. I explained how I really loved all
the bells and whistles on the Lexus; I just had to
have that raw peppiness that the Acura afforded.
Then he showed me the 350ES.

I took it for a test drive and fell in love! I made the
deal on the spot and didn't lose anything on the
trade. My salesman was awesome! He walked me
through every step, even sat and showed me
everything in the car. A week later, the owner of
the dealership called me to follow up and made
sure I liked the salesman, and that the service
department was excellent. I was amazed by this
personal phone call, but the personalization didn't
stop there!

I always trade in my cars every two years. When I
went in to see about a new one, I found a different

car that I fell in love with. There was only one drawback: it had a navigation system.

I thought there was never going to be a time in my life when I would need, much less want that feature. However, my salesman came through like a champion again. He was never pushy; he just explained the options to me. After careful consideration, we ended up buying it. The salesman said he would bring it to me. We actually took him out to dinner and he brought the car then. He's called me twice since then to make sure I still like the navigation system.

I'm not sure if the mechanical shop is in constant contact with the salesmen or if he just checks the schedule each day, but whenever we show up at the dealer's shop for our annual tune-ups, our favorite salesman is there waiting at the door with a cup of coffee to welcome us.

His ability to relate and not push his products amazes me each time and keeps bringing me back for more!

Went a Step Further
Anonymous

Sheryl and my credit union oozes in caring. She actually talks to me instead of just doing transactions. I had sold some furniture on Craig's List and was told by the buyer that he would pay the extra shipping, if I would cash his check and give him the difference.

Not really thinking about it, and it not being a major hassle, I headed off to my credit union to do so. When I got there, Sheryl started chatting with me while completing the transaction. She cashed the check for me and gave me the $2,200.

After I left, Sheryl must have thought about the transaction more and decided that something didn't feel right about it. She called the bank from which the check was drawn and checked the numbers. It turns out that the check was a fake!

She immediately started trying to hunt me down. I had just left a Western Union—having wired the money—when she called my cell phone. I was able to walk right back into that Western Union and cancel the transaction. She literally saved me $2,200. She could have ignored the fishiness and been able to say that she did exactly what I asked her to. However, Sheryl listens, she chats, she talks to customers, and she cares. She went a step further, and because of that, saved me and my family $2,200!

Helped Us in a Crisis
Paul Jones

"Our greatest asset is the customer! Treat each customer as if they are the only one!"

Laurice Leitao

I'm an avid Harley-Davidson motorcycle rider, and I have been for 30 years. However, through all of my trials and tribulations, St. Joseph Harley-Davidson and the crew ran by Mick and Clay McCreary has always come through, no matter the circumstances. One such occasion was Labor Day weekend, 2008.

My wife's boss was riding out with his wife to Colorado Springs. My wife and I decided that we would ride with them to the Colorado border, turn around, and come back. We were excited for the trip and had the bikes packed a week in advance in anticipation for our small getaway.

However, when we got about 300 miles into Kansas, disaster struck. First off, one of the bikes had oil that would spew out of the side without apparent reason. The second problem was worse: the battery wouldn't hold a charge.

We stopped at a small bike shop and bought a new battery, hoping that would fix the problem and called my service technician at St. Joe Harley— Wendell—to help us with the oil problem. Wendell gave us clear and simple directions as he walked us through the steps to fix the problem. When we got off the phone, we decided that we had better turn around and head back to St. Joseph.

However, forty miles of driving saw another dead battery. I had read in a magazine about bikers who would drive until a battery was dead, switch it with a good one off another bike, push the bike, pop the clutch, and drive until the battery was dead again.

I called St. Joseph Harley-Davidson to see if there was anything else we should try first. I spoke to Wendell again who explained that it wouldn't be a problem if we could get the bike to the dealership. So, off we went.

Every forty miles, the battery would finally drain completely and we'd have to switch it with another bike's battery and bump start it again. I kept pace on my watch, praying we would get to the dealership before it closed at 4:00 p.m. When we stopped again with a dead battery, it was 4:10. I called the dealership but no one answered.

I dug in by bike and found the dealership owner's business card. It listed his cell number and I gave it a call. Mick McCreary answered and told me that he would be at the shop when we got there. We changed the battery one last time and drove it to the dealership. When we got there, long past closing time, Mick was waiting with his wife and son.

He pushed the bike into the waiting garage and proceeded to help us unload all of the baggage, as our friends wanted to get their car and continue their trip to Colorado Springs. It was an imposition on Mick, because Saturday was the day that they have what they call a "Bike Rodeo."

On the fairgrounds outside of town, St. Joseph Harley-Davidson has food, games, and entertainment all day. Mick had obviously just left the event in order to help us out. He helped us unpack all of our items, place them into his truck, and drove us to a local motel.

He then waited until we were checked into the motel room and even helped us carry our items into the rooms. He told us if we had any other problems or needed anything to call him, and then left to go back to their rodeo.

I felt like this step went beyond what was needed. It was amazing, because he thought nothing of staying to help us unload all of our items after we checked into a motel room, even while activities were going on at the fair.

Mick and the whole St. Joseph Harley-Davidson crew really went out of their way to make sure we had safe haven. Because of that service, and their continual excellence in customer service for years, I won't buy a bike at any other dealership.

Cut the Red Tape
Aaron Quintanilla

"Customers will want to talk to you if they believe you can solve their problems."
Jeffrey Gitomer

Like most college students, I never really have more than $500 in my checking account at one time. When my account started being hit with $40 charges by companies that I'd never hear of, I of course started to overdraw my account.

I'm not sure how the companies got my card information, but after I called them, they tried to explain the "services" I was receiving in response to the charges. It was certainly nothing I would need, and definitely wasn't something I ordered. I demanded that they remove the charges and got them to admit that they would...in six to ten business days!

It was a ridiculous situation, to say the least. I hadn't bought anything; they were essentially just taking my money. I called US Bank. Naturally, I was agitated. I explained the situation and was told that if I could get the companies to fax, on their letterhead, that the charges needed to be removed, US Bank would be able to do so. Assuming that the shady companies even had letterhead, I found it bothersome, but workable.

After calling back the companies for three straight days and getting the runaround, I called US Bank back. By now, I was more than $100 in the negative and was constantly being hit with overdraft charges, further putting me into debt. When I called back, I was connected to a man by the name of John. He became my saving grace in literally ten minutes. I explained my situation and simply asked US Bank to hold off on the overdraft charges, since it certainly wasn't helping my situation. John asked me a series of three specific questions.

First, I did not authorize the charges. Next, I was not using the service. Finally, that the charges were going to be removed anyway. He then put me on hold for about 30 seconds. When he came back, he told me he had removed all the overdraft charges AND the unauthorized charges, and then proceeded to tell me my new balance. Just like that, my mess was fixed!

I was ecstatic to say the least. Like anyone, I was sick and tired of working through the problem and just wanted the hassle fixed. John did that and much more. He managed to cut through all of the red tape and just fixed the problem. I can honestly say that it was my shortest service call ever, and that it was the most effective.

Notes

1.) Can the perception by people be that you push products on them?

_____

_____

_____

_____

_____

2.) How can you cut red tape for customers?

_____

_____

_____

_____

_____

3.) Do you treat each customer as if they are your only one?

_____

_____

_____

_____

_____

A Relaxing Dinner
Cathy Christenson

Eating alone is something that very few people want to do, and something that most are uncomfortable doing. We are such a social society and the idea, frankly, scares me to death.

While attending schooling in Las Vegas for the weekend, I found myself in such a circumstance. While searching for a place to try to enjoy my meal alone, I walked into Bally's Steakhouse.

My waitress, Jennifer, was exceptional. She could clearly see my uneasiness with dining alone and sat and talked with me before asking what I would like. I asked for her recommendation, which I ordered and was not disappointed!

When I finished eating, she entertained me a while longer before saying, "To make your evening more enjoyable, I'm going to buy you dessert." A few minutes later, she brought me out a dessert!

I thoroughly enjoyed my evening. Even though she knew I was only there for a week, she gave me a very memorable dining experience. Eating alone is sometimes extremely awkward but Jennifer managed to make it a relaxing night where I enjoyed the company of an outstanding waitress!

Made My Dreams Come True
Stacy Nett

"Focus your business on what you do best. Let everyone else worry about the rest."

Kevin Stirtz

I'll be the first to admit that I'm a bit crazy about Disney. Although my dream was to be married at Disneyworld, my parents couldn't afford it, and I knew it wouldn't be reasonable to demand that from them.

Knowing my childhood dreams, my parents called Disney and asked about Mickey Mouse coming to my wedding. He couldn't make it, but the representative did tell my parents where the closest looking unlicensed costume was.

Although they couldn't send all of Mickey, the great folks at Disney did what they could and sent us a pair of Mickey's real hands for the costume.

We ended up taking a seven-day cruise and then spending another seven days in Disneyworld. When we arrived, they had everything decked out in Mickey for us! There was a wedding hat, ears, a veil, literally everything. We had a Mickey breakfast where Mickey, Minnie, Chip and Dale, Goofy, and even Pluto stopped everyone in the restaurant and married us right there.

In my home, I have a wedding certificate signed by Mickey Mouse, so he actually did my wedding! All of the great staff in Disneyworld made my dreams come true. It didn't really cost us anything extra—it was just the value of them knowing and making us fell special. They are extraordinary staff!

Adapted To Our Needs
Elise Jones

"Give what you have to somebody, it may be better than you think."
Henry Wadsworth Longfellow

I was enjoying an amazing weekend with some family in Chicago, when we decided to go to Gino's East. It's a fun restaurant where you get to write on the walls with markers and it's just a great place to eat. We were in a large group and one of the people in our party ordered a deep-dish pizza, which takes 45 minutes to cook.

The waiter, knowing this, explained and asked if we wanted our food brought out first or wanted to wait for it to all come out together. Some people piped up, said they were hungry, and wanted their salad now, and others said they would die of starvation in 45 minutes. You know, your typical large family outing.

My aunt told the waiter that we would wait; he smiled, and told us it would be right out. When he brought us our drinks back out, another guy came bearing salad and mozzarella sticks. When he tried to set them down, we told him that we didn't order that and it wasn't for us. Our waiter stepped in and said they were for us.

He explained that he had listened to us arguing over whether to wait on the food or not and so he decided to bring us out some appetizers, on him.

It was a very nice gesture and something that my aunt says happens at that restaurant all the time. That kind of service is something that doesn't take effort, just the discipline to listen to your customers and adapting to them.

From Impossible To Possible
Jenn Ray

Each year, my coworkers and I always try to get a nice birthday present for our boss. On a business trip he recently took, his iPod was crushed by a taxicab door. We decided that this year we would surprise him with a brand new iPod.

One day, he called me into his office and explained that he wanted to get an iPod to replace his broken one. He explained the color he wanted, the catchy slogan he wanted inscribed on the back, everything! I tried my best to talk him out of buying it, and as I walked away, he told me that he was going to wait until next year to get it.

I went back to my computer and sent an email to everyone explaining the conversation I just had. They all seemed excited to order the iPod— especially that we now knew exactly what he wanted.

We ordered it the next day. Five minutes later, a coworker ran to my desk screaming, "He just bought one! You placed the order and he just bought one!" After getting her to calm down, I realized that mere minutes after placing my order, our boss broke down and ordered his own.

We were devastated.

Not knowing what to do, I called Apple to see what my options were. Rose—our friendly customer service representative from Apple—listened intently to my story. When I finished the saga, she asked me to hold on for a moment. When she came back, she explained that both were already inscribed.

However, she said she got the okay from her boss to email us postage paid return address labels and cancel his order. Both would be shipped, but when his arrived, all we had to do was intercept it and mail it back to Apple. The company would take the hit on the personalized product!

Ordering it only a week before his birthday, I asked to make sure that we had paid the extra for the rushed shipping. Rose told me that we had, but that she had also removed those charges as well for all of our trouble. I almost broke down in tears!

I apologized multiple times and expressed my gratitude for her amazing solution to all of our problems.

Our boss's laser inscribed iPod arrived two days later and was shipped back. All of the charges were dropped from his credit card and we were able to give him ours on his birthday!

Rose and all of Apple personnel's dedication to customer service made an impossible situation possible.

Forgotten Sunglasses
Anonymous

"It is when we forget ourselves that we do things which will be remembered." --Anonymous

I was at a speaking engagement in Las Vegas, Nevada. I was on my way to the airport, already late for my flight and I still had to drop my car off at the rental car location. Knowing the real chance of me missing my flight, I dropped off the car, grabbed my bags, and ran to the bus that was pulling out. While standing in line at the airport security checkpoint, I noticed my cell phone was ringing. I answered the phone, only to hear a young voice who announced he was from Budget Rent-A-Car!

He told me that my sunglasses were left in the car and wanted to know if I would like them back. I of course was upset and frustrated. There was no humanly possible way for me to get back to the car drop off and make my flight. I sheepishly admitted that it was impossible for me to get back, and told him the situation. He then double checked my address from my contract and told me that they would be mailed, priority, to my house.

To say the least I was astonished and grateful for the customer service I was just presented with! When I got home, my sunglasses were already waiting for me, the postage already paid. I now have my sunglasses and I have never forgotten them again, thanks to the wonderful service that always reminds me to grab them.

Notes

1.) Do you cater you service to each customer?

_____

_____

_____

_____

2.) How will you turn the impossible into possible today?

_____

_____

_____

_____

3.) Explain how you make dreams come true.

_____

_____

_____

_____

Amazing Touches
Samantha Stickland

"Biggest question: Isn't it really 'customer helping' rather than customer service? And wouldn't you deliver better service if you thought of it that way?"

Jeffrey Gitomer

I have finally found the one place I will shop for my clothing for the rest of my life! The company's name is "myShape." The whole premise is that they predetermine clothes based on your body type.

I was a bit leery of this type of Internet company, but they sure didn't disappoint! I bought two dresses from them. It was delivered exactly when they said it would be in a beautiful package.

Each dress was contained in a gold mesh bag with a personal hand written note from the CEO of the company. Everything fit perfectly, just as they promised.

I was so delighted by the fit that I emailed them to tell them what a great experience it was and the CEO emailed me back the next day. To me, that was just an amazing touch to an amazing experience.

A Personalized Note

Anonymous

My wife and I went to Goedeker's Superstore to buy some furniture. Well actually, my wife was there to buy furniture, and I was there to smile and agree on her selection. Let's remember, it is her living room.

It took me years to figure that one out. We had to move the head of my 12-point buck out of her living room to the basement. She finally admitted to me later, "Honey, my girlfriends found the head of a deer in my living room tacky." Notice the word "my" living room. There are some things not worth fighting. Who owns the living room is one of them. Smile and nod.

When she makes the final nod of approval, I know it's safe to reply, "Honey that is exactly the piece I wanted the whole time." If she sighs, smiles and scrunches her shoulders in that cute way she does, I know I'm home free. If she hasn't made her decision yet and I slip my line too early, I could be sleeping on the couch we're about to buy.

Anyway, as we're looking, Steve Goedeker personally helped us that day. Although we didn't make a selection that day—a whole other story— two days later we received a note in the mail. As I picked it up to read it, I noticed it was a personalized thank you note from Mr. Goedeker himself, thanking us for coming in to look at his selections.

Drove In From Home

Jessica Muhm

My best service comes from a place that leaves little in the way of needed service: a tanning salon.

I was getting ready to have some pictures taken with the family and was going to have a spray tan applied so I had that bronzed, summer look.

When I went to the tanning salon I had picked out, everything was dark and there was a closed sign over the door. I checked the times on the door, and according to my watch, unless it was five hours slow, the shop should still be open.

There was no one in the shop, but I called the number on the door, just in case they had it forwarded. Sure enough, a lady answered. I explained the situation, and my thoughts that the shop should have still been open. She replied, "Oh my, I apologize, I didn't repost my new hours for the new year."

She then had me hold on while she drove in to the shop from home and helped us with all of our services. I expected the, "Those aren't our hours anymore" response, but was pleasantly surprised by her willingness to drive back, just to serve our needs.

Stayed Late
Jennifer Cook

"Memorable customer service can only take place in a human-to-human situation."

Jeffrey Gitomer

Our local bank always holds craft days around special holidays. They have one for Mother's Day, Father's Day, and even around back to school time. It's a time when children can come into the store and make a craft for someone, free of charge.

Several years ago, when my girls were one and two, my husband took them to the bank for their Mother's Day Craft Day. He, however, misread the flyer on the refrigerator and by the time he got there, the craft time was over and everyone was gone, except for a few employees.

As they walked into the lobby, he tried to explain his mistake to the girls and tell them that they could do something else for Mommy. A teller overheard him. She walked over, got down to the girls' level and said, "I think we have some extra supplies left over. Why don't I go take you and you can go ahead and make the craft for your Mom?"

This was a Saturday at about four o'clock. It was well outside of the normal banking hours, and a time when most employees just want to go home. However, the employee took my children to the area and allowed them to make the craft for me.

She even came back with cookies that were left over from the snacks the bank provided.

They had run out of drinks, but the tellers took the time to buy each girl a juice from the vending machine. The girls probably spent 45 minutes to an hour making the craft, but the tellers were happy to stay and help them, as each girl took her time to make the perfect present.

It was great of them to not only to make the offer, but to also follow through and wait for the girls to make everything after hours. She provided them with treats out of the vending machine, even though they were late. It made an impact on my husband and I and we still bank there for that very reason.

Focused On Me and My Problem
Tom Hille

"Nobody can prevent you from choosing to be exceptional."
Mark Sanborn

Last summer I traveled through Europe with my wife and we stayed at a number of different hotels. The one that I remember as better than the rest is the Eden Hotel Wolff in Munich, Germany.

One event that particularly sticks in my mind was while I was trying to print our boarding passes for the next day's travel. The printer indicated that it was low on toner. I went to the front desk and spoke to the attendant who immediately came over and tried what people usually try: shaking the container. She ended up with toner all over the place. The end had opened up and it exploded everywhere!

As I was apologizing for the trouble, and she was apologizing to me for all the mess, she said, "No, let's go to my office and we'll use my computer and printer." She took me to her office behind the coveted front desk. She sat at the keyboard, retyped everything in for me, and printed out my boarding passes in no time at all.

During that time, it was the only thing on my mind. To me, that was exceptional, that she only focused on my problem and me.

Notes

1.) How do you help customers?

_____

_____

_____

_____

_____

2.) How can you personalize every interaction you have with a customer today?

_____

_____

_____

_____

_____

3.) Will you chose to be exceptional today?

_____

_____

_____

_____

Took Ownership of Our Event
Danielle Easton

My high school had the amazing opportunity to host Missouri's Student Council State Convention. While exploring different venues to hold the advisor luncheon, I stumbled across the Holiday Inn Conference Center.

With scheduling both the student and advisors lunches, I had to be in two locations at one time. This daunting task started to frighten me, as the date loomed closer. However, the more I worked with the outstanding staff at the Holiday Inn, the more relaxed I became.

The only problem we had was the price per lunch. After discussing this with them, they told us that it was already taken care of. When we cut the check, I realized that the hotel had given us the food at cost. They had completely removed their commission! That was just the start.

Our hotel contact volunteered her time to help us decorate, picked out the decorations, even down to the food titles, which matched our Las Vegas theme. When I walked in there were balloons and even piñatas hanging from the ceiling. Their actions took so much stress off me and allowed me to enjoy my time at the conference as well. We ended up being provided with a $30 lunch for only $9.

Never Gave Us an Excuse
Anonymous

*"One customer well taken care of could be more valuable
than $10,000 worth of advertising."*

Jim Rohn

I don't usually eat at Hardees. Not that I particularly mind it, but it just never has been my first choice in fast food. However, my wife and I found ourselves eating there.

We were in a rush, and found it to be the only fast food on the block without a line. After we placed our order, we realized that there was one person working behind the counter. He was working the front and the drive-thru with one person actually making the burgers in the back.

After placing our order we waited, waited, and waited. It took a long time for our food to get to us. Eventually our food arrived and he apologized for the delay.

We said it was no problem but later on, he came back out to apologize again and promised us a milkshake if we wanted one. We didn't really have the time for it, but we've been back to Hardees twice since then. He never gave an excuse or told us they were short staffed, which they obviously were. He just apologized for the long wait and offered us a complimentary shake for our trouble.

Gift Wrapped Surprise
Amy Beaumont

"The most important adage and the only adage is, the customer comes first, whatever the business, the customer comes first."

Kerry Stokes

Late one afternoon, I needed to get a gift for my manager who was retiring the next day.

I didn't have much time, so on my lunch break I stopped by a local jewelry store to see if I could pick something up. They were kind enough to agree to engrave a watch for me by the end of the day.

The jeweler delivered the gift to my office on time, gift wrapped for me with a ribbon ready to attach my personalized note. They came through for me in a pinch with the perfect gift with impossibly short notice.

Used Common Sense
Carlos Villegas

"The biggest reason that positive endings don't happen is because employees are trained on policies and rules rather than principles."
Jeffrey Gitomer

A few years ago, I had a cell phone plan through Cingular Wireless. With two lines, I covered my sister and myself. When my sister's phone was stolen, I called and cancelled her phone, not thinking anything of it.

When my bill came for that month, it was extremely high. I called Cingular's customer service department to inquire about the bill. I was told that it was due to calls made to Africa. I prepared myself to the inevitable argument to have them removed.

I explained how the phone was stolen and that I didn't make the calls. I started to get defensive about the situation when the representative told me not to worry. He removed the charges immediately and blocked the phone for international calls.

Once it was all over, I felt relieved and happy. A phone call that I expected to take an hour took a mere fifteen minutes. After explaining the situation, the agent didn't ask for more details because it was common sense—which is very rare to find these days.

Created Happiness
Mark Arnold

"Every company's greatest assets are its customers, because without customers there is no company."
Michael LeBoeuf

For our family vacation one year, my wife and I decided to take our two young girls to the Walt Disney World Resort in Florida. You know: princesses, palaces, shows, rides, etc. Everyone has to experience the Disney vacation at least once in their life with their kids. It is a magical place.

Since this was a "once in a lifetime" vacation we even stayed at one of the Disney resort properties, Fort Wilderness. Disney's brand slogan is, "We create happiness," and boy did we ever experience it!

My oldest daughter's most prized possession in life was a blanket we gave her when she was born. She called it her "animal blankey" because it was white and adorned with colorful animal pictures.

Each day we would leave our hotel room and enjoy the wonderful Disney parks. Whether it was riding "It's a Small World," watching the Little Mermaid show or having a meal with one of the many Disney characters, we were having a family blast.

Each day Elizabeth would leave animal blankey neatly tucked away our hotel room. Of course, every day a maid would clean our room. One evening we returned from a fun-filled day at the Magic Kingdom. The first thing Elizabeth looked for was animal blankey. To her shock and dismay, (not to mention her parents) the blanket was gone! In her haste to clean our room, the maid accidently took animal blankey. My daughter's most prized position in life was missing.

We immediately called the property manager. He went through lost and found. He contacted the cleaning crew. No animal blankey. It turned out that ALL the laundry in ALL the Disney properties is shipped off-site to a special facility. Somewhere in that massive sea of white sheets, pillowcases and blankets was my daughter's lifeguard.

That was when we had to have "the talk" with our daughter. The "sometimes things in life just happen" talk.

Our vacation eventually ended. The day after we got home, we received a call from Disney. They had found "animal blankey!" They had gone through mounds and mounds of dirty laundry to find one little girl's blanket. They said they would be shipping it to us overnight. When it arrived the next morning, it was freshly washed.

Why in the world would a business do this? It's just as if they told me on the phone. They create happiness.

Notes

1.) Are you result or excuse driven?

_____
_____
_____
_____
_____

2.) Are you trained on policy or principle?

_____
_____
_____
_____
_____

3.) What is your company's greatest asset?

_____
_____
_____
_____
_____

Provided Assistance
Carolyn Jordan

"Customer service is just a day in, day out ongoing, never ending, unremitting, persevering, compassionate, type of activity."
Leon Gorman, CEO, L.L.Bean

We tend to overvalue youth in our society. Whether it is advertisers targeting their messages to the coveted 18 to 35-year-old demographic or brands touting "look and feel younger," aging consumers are treated differently.

But at my credit union, Neighborhood Credit Union, their saying is "world-class service, neighborhood convenience." Not "world-class service if you're under 40" but "world-class service." I have seen them put this into action a few times.

The first story was when the Social Security Administration (SSA) made an error with one of their members (Mrs. Miller). The SSA reported the member as being deceased and stopped her direct deposit. Obviously, when Mrs. Miller found out she was dead, she was a little upset!

The credit union arranged a conference call with the member, the Social Security Administration and the credit union office. But the SSA said since the matter involved someone who was "deceased" they required the person appear in person at their offices.

Unfortunately, Mrs. Miller was almost 80 years old and recovering from hip surgery. So the credit union call center representative that had been helping Mrs. Miller, went to her home, drove her to the SSA office, assisted her in resolving the matter and even took Mrs. Miller to lunch on the way home!

The second illustration comes from one of my own experiences. Mrs. Jones had been a member of our credit union since 1956. She was 85-years-old when she came in and requested eight years worth of statements in order to see if a family member had repaid her on a loan.

I told her it would be my pleasure to mail them the next day. In the process of talking with her however, I realized that she was living in a retirement community just a mile away.

Instead of putting them in the next day's mail, I dropped by her house on my way home from work that day.

We talked for quite some time and I could see that she was very glad to have some company. The next time our credit union held an event, I made sure that she was mailed a personalized invitation and was ecstatic when she showed up. Sometimes the best service isn't what you receive, but what you can give.

Upbeat And Friendly
Robin Skelly

"Nothing is so contagious as enthusiasm."
                                    Samuel Taylor Coleridge

How many times have you called a computer company for technical support only to learn you're talking to someone a million miles away? It doesn't exactly endear you to the company. You're already frustrated and mad that things aren't working. Now you have to try and communicate with someone whose accent is a barrier.

While this is a typical experience for most, I experienced something completely difference with Netgear, a computer router company.

I had to call their customer service department because the router wasn't working. I was immediately put on hold for five minutes. It was bad enough that my Internet wasn't working, but now I had to wait on hold!

Already annoyed, I hear from E.J. next. Located in the Philippines, he started the conversation with a friendly and upbeat, "Hello Ma'am!" He was probably standing up and moving around he was so happy and full of energy.

He used my name consistently throughout the conversation, even relating my name to "Robin Hood." Through the course of the call, E.J. put me at east by asking where I was from, how long I had lived there, asking about the weather and engaging me in conversation.

He patiently walked me through the technical issues step by step; all the while being slow and patient. He even told me, "You're so fast, you're a genius. You'll be in the Guinness Book of World Records." I was a genius because E.J. told me I was.

While fixing the problem, he gave me personal details about his life. He explained he lived in the Philippines and was looking forward to celebrating his one-year anniversary with his girlfriend later that night.

He made me laugh the whole time, constantly keeping me entertained. Although the call only lasted ten minutes, he summarized everything for me, gave me a reference call, and ended our powerful exchange.

What started as a potentially frustrating customer service issue turned into a great one!

A Part Of The Family
Anonymous

"You can't expect your employees to exceed the expectations of your customers if you don't exceed the employees' expectations of manage."
Howard Schultz, CEO Starbucks Coffee

I had been working for Marriott for about six months when my father had passed away. As usual, I took time off to grieve and go through that process.

The very next day I received calls from my management asking if everything was alright. My mother even received calls making sure that she was okay! For the next week, we received catered meals provided free of charge from the hotel.

There was never any pressure to come back, get back to the job, or anything. Even after I came back, my managers sat me down to make sure that I was okay. They told me that I could take six weeks or more if I needed it.

I replied that I honestly couldn't sit at home alone anymore, but they were genuinely concerned and cared about me as a person, not just a worker. Their care made me feel like I was a part of the Marriott family, and is a feeling I've never received from any other employer.

A Welcomed Difference
Colleen Cormier

In my opinion, purchasing a car ranks up there with having a root canal. Haggling over the right price, getting the run-around from a sales representative and the overall pressure to sell you a vehicle on the spot don't come anywhere close to what I would consider enjoyable—or even bearable! Naturally, when my husband came home from work one day and insisted I accompany him to Metroplex Toyota in Duncanville, Texas, I wanted to pretend I didn't hear him.

We had barely just recovered from our experience at a different dealership days before. At that dealership we found a sales representative who was only interested in his commission. Our test drive was less than a mile since the truck was low on gas and almost ran out on us! To make it worse, we wanted a green automatic, but we were pushed to buy a white manual since that was all they had on the lot that day. Needless to say, I wasn't interested in a double root canal.

Insisting that Metroplex was different, my husband explained he had stopped on the way home from work, took a test drive, and couldn't say enough for them. I took the bait and met him there the following day.

It was everything you don't expect in a car dealership, but should. Danny, our sales

98

representative, escorted us to his office, offered us a beverage and asked us about our needs, all the while listening attentively and taking notes. He then searched the database to find the exact truck my husband wanted.

Even though there wasn't one on the lot, Danny said he could get it there in a reasonable amount of time. He even apologized for not having the right color on the lot and asked our permission to test drive the same model in a different color!

It was the road test of a lifetime. Allowing us to drive it for at least 30 minutes, we drove on the highway, stop-and-go traffic, even rocks and dirt! Danny told us that if we were going to buy a truck, we should be able to experience everything it was made to do. And we did. By the end of our visit, we were completely sold—without any pressure. In fact, Danny even asked if we needed to take a day or two to think about it. I had to pinch myself to be sure he really asked us that question. No pressure? Not even haggling?

The delivery was just as incredible. Showing us all the gadgets and gizmos in the truck, Danny didn't just demonstrate, he allowed us to try it to be sure that we would remember it. It was the first time in our lives we didn't have to spend a month studying the owner's manual.

From the greeting at the door, to the smooth financing process, and everything in between, I was just wowed beyond belief.

Quickly Adapted
James Frankeberger

"The customer is king."

Unknown

Sometimes your boss gives you a tangible example of the best service you can provide. Although our chef picks out fresh fish from the local sea market right off the coast, we still have requests that we've never thought of.

When requesting our dessert menu, a large party noticed that we did not have sherbet ice cream. They really enjoyed the dinner, but they were disappointed that we did not have any on our menu. My store manager had me run to the grocery store down the street to purchase the sherbet ice cream. He insisted that we serve them, free of charge, when I returned.

They were utterly impressed with how we quickly responded to their needs and became very loyal to the restaurant. It made an impression on me and how I looked at serving customers from that point forward.

Notes

1.) How does your voice and posture diffuse anger?

_____

_____

_____

_____

_____

2.) How do you make your customers a king?

_____

_____

_____

_____

_____

3.) Are your customers part of your corporate family?

_____

_____

_____

_____

_____

A Little Extra
Janet Sanders

"Choose to deliver amazing service to your customers. You'll stand out because they don't get it anywhere else."
Kevin Stirtz

Great service often means doing something unexpected for the customer. Fast food chains are not often recognized for providing superior service or extra nice touches with your meal. However, at a Taco Bell in Louisiana they did just that.

I was traveling on business and stopped at a Taco Bell drive-thru. Of course Mexican food can be a bit messy, and you typically get the standard three or four napkins in your bag. By the time you realize you don't have enough, you're already fifteen minutes down the road and certainly aren't going to turn around.

But as I pulled away, I opened my bag to make sure all of my purchases were there, and saw a special surprise. Sitting on top of my three soft tacos was a finger wipe towelette! It touched me as just something useful and special. It was a little extra touch that made the difference to me on that day.

Although I've had complimentary meals thanks to mistakes in the kitchen, it was the smallest hand wipe that is my best service story.

Saw My Stress
Tracy Long

Thanksgiving can be a stressful time a year. Getting the house ready for company, cooking the perfect meal, entertaining relatives. And yes, buying the right turkey.

When I received a coupon in the mail from Kroger Grocery Store for a free 16-pound turkey, I knew where I was going to get my turkey this year. For me, 16-pounds was just the right size.

When I got there, I started hunting through the "turkey freezer" searching for a 16-pound turkey. I was determined to find a 16-pounder. After all, no 16-pounds, no free turkey.

Fortunately, one of the meat butchers saw my dilemma. The elderly gentleman walked up to me and said, "Sweetheart, are you looking for one of those 16-pound turkeys?" I meekly nodded yes.

"Well they don't exist." He charmingly proceeded to help me pick out a 20-pound turkey. Telling me the cashier would work it out for me at the front, he sent me on my way! He even put it in the cart for me!

If it weren't for the butcher and his incredible attitude I would still be at Kroger digging through their turkeys!

Gave Us Sound Advice
Maria Monroy

"Would you do business with you?"
Linda Silverman Goldzimer

USAA, a financial service provider, is known for its superior service. It was no different when my husband and I were shopping for a used car. The rates were high at all the banks we checked with and the car dealership, so we decided to call USAA.

The representative I spoke with was more than patient. He explained all the financing options and even helped us by looking up the price of the car. We were actually able to lower the price of the vehicle because he gave us such great information!

He also went on to help me, and not just increase their bottom line, by telling me how we could pay off the loan quicker with lower payments. I was even helped with our budget and long-term goals by making more payments. They actually gave us advice!

It wasn't like we were doing business. Hearing the kind of information we did from someone lending us the money made it so reassuring.

Although we were on the phone for close to 45 minutes, he never seemed to be in a rush. Extremely patient and focused on me, I felt like I was being helped.

Became A Tradition
Theresa Wolff

*"When you serve the customer better, there's always a
return on your investment."*
Kara Parlin

A few years ago, my husband made reservations
for a special anniversary dinner for us at Antoine's
Restaurant in the New Orleans French Quarter.
Initially I was a bit uncomfortable at the thought
of dining in an establishment that looked old,
pretentious and quite frankly, stuffy. I thought I
might be made to feel like I was intruding in a
place I didn't belong.

However, we were instead greeted warmly at the
front door by the smiling hostess who called us by
name. After we were seated, our server Greg,
chatted with us about why we were here, how long
we had been married and if we had any children.
Armed with that information, he waived for the
"wine guy," whispered something to him, and he
scurried off. Greg continued by explaining the
daily specials. When the wine guy came back, he
was bearing a tray with two glasses of champagne
and an appetizer, "compliments of the house" as
Greg put it.

That's when they had me. I no longer felt like an
outsider. I felt special.

The rest of the evening was just as special as the
first five minutes. Everyone who served us called
us by name. From the man who filled up our

water, to the guy who scraped the crumbs from the tablecloth. Everyone was so friendly and made us feel very comfortable in a restaurant that I thought might be too pretentious to be relaxing.

At the end of dinner, Greg came with the dessert menus. Although we thought we were too full, his ability to explain desserts, and this one in particular, we couldn't resist.

He explained the history of the restaurant and how the dessert was a part of that history. He wasn't pushy, he just explained it completely, and gave it his personal endorsement!

After wheeling the cart containing all the necessary ingredients, he whipped up this famous flaming concoction at our table! It was certainly one of the most wonderful culinary experiences we have ever had. But even more than that, it was our most memorable meal—because of the service.

Of course we went back for our next anniversary and plan to continue to make it a tradition. Although we don't always get Greg, the service is impeccable, no matter whom you have.

Never Pressured Me
Eve Hernandez

"Whatever your business is, talk to your customers and provide them with what they want. It makes sense."
Robert Bowman

My most recent great service experience was at the Kiehl's counter at Saks Fifth Avenue. It's an upscale retail center in San Antonio, Texas. I try to avoid these high-end stores since I just don't have that 'fashionista' look. Instead I have the 'Weekend Apparel Trifecta'—if my clothes are clean, match, and fit—then I'm good. Since my clothes don't scream that I'm going to spend a lot of money, I usually don't get a lot of help unless I jump up and flail my arms in the air.

But on this occasion, I succumbed to the latest trend and was in search of a specific moisturizer. So off I went in jeans, no makeup, with two crabby kids in tow.

I was eyeing the glass cases at Kiehl's to find my moisturizer and leave before my kids made a mess of the lip balm and cold cream samples. A nice young man walked up and asked if he could help me. In my desperation to get out, I grumbled the name of the product I needed.

He smiled and replied, "Yes, for your complexion. That can be very hard to maintain, especially in this weather." He asked if I would like to try a sample and let it dry before buying it. Reluctantly, I took him up on his offer.

As I sat at the counter, he engaged my daughters in conversation, offered them samples of creams, shampoos and conditioners. He even wrapped them up in tissue paper like expensive treasures and placed them in a very sturdy paper shopping bag.

I was sold. I bought the moisturizer, matching cleanser, toner, scrub, hydrating mask and even the promotional rubber duck, just because we were having so much fun!

Each product was described to me, I was given the chance to use it, was given a money-back guarantee and even an offer to come in for a free facial at the cosmetic section of the boutique. The representative never pressured me to buy anything, only to try the products. When I turned down a tea tree oil scrub that I knew I didn't need or want, there was no insistence on his part that I needed to use the product or suffer the consequences years down the road.

I went from dreading this experience to relishing it and telling all my family about it. I use the products every day, and I usually recall the original purchase, which always makes me smile. Kiehl's has a customer for life, and I'll go 36 miles round-trip to the Saks Fifth Avenue across town to get more.

Notes

1.) What do your customers receive from you
that they don't get anywhere else?

_____

_____

_____

_____

_____

2.) Do you listen to your customers to see what
they want before talking?

_____

_____

_____

_____

_____

3.) Would you send a customer to another
store if they had a product you did not?

_____

_____

_____

_____

_____

Searched for Entertainment
Jennifer Cook

I have two girls, five and four. When you go to a restaurant, especially at that age, you have to find kid friendly places. When we got to On The Border, one of their favorite places, the host took us to our seats with the children's menu. They were of course the kind that you can draw on with crayons.

But when he sat us down, there weren't any crayons waiting. Although I normally bring extra pens for them, I had forgot them at home.

I stopped another host and asked if they had any pens or pencils that the kids could use. Before that host came back, our original host who seated us came back with dry erase markers in his hand. He leaned down to the girls' level and asked, "Will these work for you?" They were of course excited about them.

We made it a point to make sure we returned the pens when we left so that the next child would have something to color with. But it was very important to me that the host went out of his way and thought outside of mere pencils and pens to find dry erase markers for my kids to be entertained with.

Showed a Personal Concern
Vickey Morris

"There's a place in this world for any business that takes care of its customers after the sale."

Harvey Mackay

A hailstorm blew through Carrollton, Texas during the spring of 2008 and managed to remove several sets of shingles from my roof.

I immediately contacted my insurance company who assigned an adjuster to come take a look at the roof. Much to my surprise, I was told the damage was not bad enough to merit the replacement of the roof and the repairs weren't even enough to meet my deductible!

Knowing that something had to be done about it, I called roofers to get an estimate on the cost to replace the roof. Although every one of the companies I called was a professional, I felt like one individual—Scott—had my best interests in mind.

Scott first asked if I needed an emergency repair to my roof. There was another set of storms coming through that weekend and he was worried about additional damage to both the external and internal parts of my house.

He was out that very same morning and made the emergency repairs so that I could at least weather the storms headed our way. I asked how much for this quick fix, and he told me not to worry about it.

111

Scott then blew me away when he told me that he couldn't understand why the insurance company was not going to completely replace the roof. He proceeded to coach me on what I needed to contest the insurance's decision and force them to send a second adjuster to look at the roof.

Scott even came to my house the day the adjuster was there and represented me as he made his evaluation.

I received a total of four estimates. Scott wasn't the lowest, but he also wasn't the highest. Because of his diligent work, I not only got a new roof, but they replaced half of my window screens because of the damage from the storm. My only out of pocked expense was just my deductible.

Although Scott saved me $5,000 that day, he saved himself a whole lot more by gaining all of my business. He showed a personal concern for my situation from the first phone call.

From Horrible to Honorable

James Robert Lay

"The purpose of business is to create and keep a customer."
Peter Drucker

As a young entrepreneur and web-marketing consultant, I travel frequently to visit clients, attend conferences and speak at different events. Along with the travel come airline flights, car rentals, restaurants and hotel stays, each offering their own service experience story. Some have been good. Some have been bad. Some have been lost in the shuffle.

However, there is one event that stands out in my mind, which may have started as a horrible hotel experience, but one individual took the time to provide my best service ever.

It all began in April of 2006 when I attended an annual meeting in Austin, Texas. As I was exhibiting at the event's vendor expo, I drove in late from Houston the night before the conference began. My reservations were made for the Hilton Garden Inn, down the street from event's location.

Upon arriving, I left my car with the valet. While they unpacked my car, the valet offered to hold any items I had for the conference. One of the items was a boxed 32" LCD TV that was part of my vendor expo display. I was handed my claim ticket and helped to my room for the evening.

Upon waking in the morning, full of excitement for the day's events, I quickly dressed and made my way to the lobby for breakfast. As I sipped a cup of coffee, I gave my claim ticket to the valet to retrieve my vendor expo items for the conference. However, to my disbelief, the valet returned to inform me that they could not find my LCD TV anywhere!

Slow to anger, I asked to speak to the hotel manager. She assured me they would find the TV. I explained what the television would be used for and how the conference would start in less than an hour.

Extremely upset and disappointed, I was given her card and cell phone number while another valet helped me over to the conference center. Once again, she reassured me that she would do everything she could to help me out and would call me on my cell to keep me updated.

As I was setting up my booth at the expo, my cell phone rang, and the hotel manager asked to get a few more details about the TV including the size and brand. She told me she would call me back in a few minutes after researching the issue further. By now, it was 10:00 a.m., the conference was starting and people were beginning to enter the expo hall.

By 10:30 a.m., she arrived to personally deliver a new TV, bought at Best Buy, to the expo hall and even helped me set it up!

Replacements Even Years Later

Fred Brown

"The goal as a company is to have customer service that is not just the best, but legendary."

Sam Walton

My outstanding customer service story takes place at a retail location known for superior customer service, so this is no surprise.

I had purchased a pair of slippers at L.L. Bean and had comfortably worn them for about four years. I wore these slippers inside and outside when running to get the newspaper or the mail. They were great!

One day, while sloshing through a puddle, I noticed my left big toe getting a bit nippy, as cold water seeped in to the slipper. I called L.L. Bean to order another pair, and when they asked where I heard of them, I said that I had a pair now and I needed another one.

I recounted the story, and the L.L. Bean representative told me they would give me another pair. All I had to do was send the slippers back to them and they would send me a new pair. She said it was because they considered the slippers to be "defective" even after four years of wear.

Needless to say, I shipped them back and received another pair a couple weeks later. I have continued to shop at L.L Bean because of this one experience.

Fixed our Sprayer
Kim McGriff

"The customer is why you go to work. If they go away, you do, too."

David Haverford

Several years ago, when Lowe's had just opened in the area, my husband and I spent a Saturday morning there getting materials to work in our yard. We bought mulch and flowers, some stain for our bridge and a sprayer. We went home, unloaded our stuff and started working. Several hours later, we were both just covered in dirt.

When it was time to spray the bridge, we encountered a problem. The sprayer wouldn't work. I couldn't believe it. I was filthy and tired. I didn't want to clean myself up just to go back to Lowe's, because I wasn't finished working in the yard. And, I was so dirty I couldn't even get in my car.

Frustrated, I called Lowe's to tell them my situation. They actually sent someone to my house with a replacement sprayer. I was shocked! I don't know if they'd still do that today, but I was very impressed.

Notes

1.) How do you fix things when they are wrong?

_____

_____

_____

_____

_____

2.) Why do *you* go to work?

_____

_____

_____

_____

_____

3.) Name ways to make your service legendary:

_____

_____

_____

_____

_____

Remembered Our Quirks
Jennifer Hill

*"Customer service is training people how to serve
clients in an outstanding fashion."*

Unknown

There's an On The Border restaurant near my
house, and one day my family decided to eat there
for dinner. There are five of us in my family –
myself, my husband, and my three kids – and for a
while my brother was living with us. So, six of us
walked in to the restaurant, and we are big people,
so we definitely stand out when we go somewhere.

We are also a family that is very specific about
what we want. We don't order anything the way it
is on the menu. My brother never drinks ice in his
drinks. My son always gets milk no matter where
we go. I don't like jalapenos on my seven-layer dip,
etc. We ordered accordingly, ate our meal, and
went home. The service was okay.

About a month later, the restaurant was having a
promotion where you get an appetizer, entrée and
dessert for a flat fee. Like I said, we're a big family
both in number and size, so we headed back over
to On the Border and happened to get seated with
the same server we had the first time we were
there.

Not even two minutes after we were seated, he
brought out all of our drinks, without us even
ordering them, and they were exactly the way we

like them – no ice in my brother's drink, extra lemon in my tea, milk for my son and so on. Then, he proceeded to ask us if we'd like the same appetizers we ordered last time, prepared the same way we had asked for them last time.

We had only seen this guy once, and a month later, he remembered us like we had been there yesterday. This guy blew me away. He was just phenomenal. He remembered everything to a tee, and to be able to get that type of service was a real treat.

Knew My Name
Allison Griffin

When we relocated to Dallas and were beginning construction on a new home, I was seeking a way to send only one change of address to all our friends, since we would live in a rental property for a few months until we could move into our permanent new home.

I contacted the U.S. Postal Service to find out whether we could establish a mailbox and mailing address at a construction site. After several phone calls and quite a few hoops, the Postmaster for my location told me that it was at the mail carrier's discretion. So I left a phone message for my future mail carrier, Bob.

When we finally connected, he heard my request and graciously agreed to start delivering mail to a home under construction. He even contacted me when there were packages and once drove one over to my rental house. He has served my particular street for more than 15 years and is on a first-name basis with me and many of my neighbors, which makes his service pretty remarkable.

Bob is a busy person with MANY customers but he took the time to learn my name and remember details about my life. What a huge difference that makes, and it makes me into a very loyal customer!

Ease and Convenience
Kathi Dodd

"It is in this moment you have the power to be the solution!"

Ileana Kane

A few years ago, I made my mother-in-law a calendar on my computer using pictures of my family. She loved it so much that she wanted another one the following year. Unfortunately, I never got around to making it. I decided that for Christmas this year, I'd use one of those online services where I can insert the pictures and pay them to print it. That would save me time, give her a nice quality gift and have it shipped directly to her home.

That was the plan until she called out of the blue one day and announced they would be coming to visit two days later to celebrate Christmas with us a little early. I immediately got online to see where I could make a calendar that would be ready in two days. Nobody would do it.

The normal drug stores that offer one-hour photo processing all print their calendars elsewhere and required a lead-time of two weeks. After much searching, I had resigned myself to the fact that she would not have a gift to open at my house. It would have to be shipped, and I wouldn't get to see the look on her face when she saw all of those pictures on a beautiful calendar.

The next day, I was watching a Christmas special on television with my son when a commercial came on for Ritz camera. After advertising the cameras that were on sale, the commercial said I could go to ritzpix.com, make a photo calendar online and print it within an hour, just like one-hour photo processing. I wasn't sure I heard that correctly, so I went online to check it out.

Sure enough, it was true. They had beautiful calendar templates, and I already had my photos picked. All I had to do was pick which photos I wanted to place on which pages. I made the entire calendar in 20 minutes, set it up to print at a Ritz camera just down the street from my house and had the option of paying online or paying when I picked it up in the store.

I chose to pay at the store so I could examine the quality of the finished product before purchasing it. Less than an hour after I hit "submit" on my order, I received an e-mail saying my calendar had been printed and was ready for pick-up. This was at 10:00 at night.

The next morning I drove to the store, walked right up to the counter and picked up my calendar. It took five minutes to get in and out of the store, and I left with a beautiful, high-quality gift for my mother-in-law that I was able to watch her open and enjoy. It was the highlight of my holidays, and I couldn't be more grateful to Ritz camera for making something special so easy and convenient.

Where Are You Headed?

Anonymous

"If you want to lift yourself up, lift up someone else."
Booker T. Washington

I want to share an outstanding—and very amusing—customer service experience I had on a flight.

I flew Southwest Airlines from San Jose to Denver on one day in August. The flight was about to board when I decided I needed dinner.

Knowing I had a few minutes, because I was in boarding group "B", I rushed over to Burger King, keeping a careful eye on the gate.

Group "A" boarded.

The Burger King line was moving slowly and I resigned myself to the fact that I did not have enough time to get my meal. I turned around to leave, nearly running into a tall, uniformed man.

"Where are you headed?" he asked. "Denver?"

"Yes," I replied.

"Don't worry. I won't leave without you," he said reassuringly.

"Oh, you're the pilot." I said, stating the obvious. I settled back into line, keeping an eye on the gate. Group "B" was boarding.

123

"You know," the pilot said, "Why don't you give me your receipt and go get on the plane. I'll bring you your meal."

Surprised and grateful, I rushed to my place in line. I boarded in the correct position and settled into my window seat.

Not ten minutes later, a flight attendant asked over the loudspeaker, "Mary, can you raise your hand? We have your meal." My burger and fries were delivered to my seat.

I can honestly say this was one of the nicest and most surprising things that happened to me on a flight, ever. I just want to thank the pilot, the flight attendant, and Southwest for cultivating a culture where employees go out of their way to surprise and delight their customers.

Fixed Their Mistake
Teresa Mann

I had a conference that I was attending in San Diego many years ago when I received service that I will never forget.

The hotel—a Marriott—overbooked the hotel. So they were forced to ship me, very late at night, to another Marriott a few blocks away. This would have been fine, but this was not where the conference was being held, and certainly not my first choice.

When I arrived at the hotel, I was provided with $250 in cash for the night. I received a call the next morning telling me that there was room at the conference hotel and they would shuttle a car and get my bags brought right over.

When I arrived, I was put into a suite and had a complimentary fruit basket waiting on me. Sitting with the basket was a nice letter saying that the night at the hotel was on them and I could also keep the $250 for all of my trouble.

It was a touch that was so over the top that I felt more than served, I felt like I was taking advantage of them.

Notes

1.) How do you implement courtesy in daily interactions with customers?

_____

_____

_____

_____

_____

2.) Do you watch those around you close enough to know their fears?

_____

_____

_____

_____

_____

3.) With your customers, how are you the solution?

_____

_____

_____

_____

_____

Best At A Value

Terry Templeton

"A customer is the most important visitor on our premises.
He is not dependent on us – we are dependent on him."
Unknown

Some people feel that to get outstanding service, you have to stay at the most expensive hotels. That's not always the case.

While talking with some friends at a party, they explained their plan to ride their motorcycles down to Arkansas for a Blues and Bar-B-Q festival. I was interested and eagerly checked my calendar when I got home. Seeing nothing on it, I checked with the wife and started packing my bags.

I called my friends back to check on the date and find out what motel they were staying at. Knowing the hundreds of bikers that would be visiting the festival, I immediately got online and booked a room at the Value Place Motel in Springdale, Arkansas, where they were staying.

The next day I received a call saying the computer system had screwed up and accidently booked me for a room when they didn't have any available. However, I was told that the Value Place in Bentonville, Arkansas had plenty of room and was given the number. I called and reserved a room for myself.

As we rode through Arkansas, we discovered that their motel room and mine were separated by fifteen miles. It was certainly an inconvenience.

When we got to their motel for them to check in, I mentioned to the lady behind the counter my appreciation that she called. I knew that if she had not have called, I certainly would not have found a room.

She then told me that they had five cancellations that day. Volunteering to call my motel and arrange to have my reservation switched, I began filling out all of the necessary paperwork.

We ended up switching motels. It was a great weekend and staying so close to our friends made it even nicer. Even though we were staying at the Value Place, our expectations were exceeded tenfold and were provided with outstanding service!

Helped Me Gain My Calm
Steve Bryant

"Successful people are always looking for opportunities to help others. Unsuccessful people are always asking, 'What's in it for me?'"

Brian Tracy

Everyone has those times in their life when they fear the unthinkable. They remember exactly where they left something, only to discover that it is not there when they return. This exact circumstance happened to me on a recent conference I attended.

I had placed my bag, containing my personal items, including my keys, phone and important documents in the conference room and stepped outside to grab a quick drink before the session started.

When I returned, I almost fell into a panic when I realized my bag was gone! There were others from my work attending the session, and I asked each of them if they had seen it. All replied it wasn't there when they walked in.

I immediately started to canvas the gigantic room to see if someone had picked it up accidentally. No luck. In my frantic search and look of horror I'm sure was on my face, the concierge from the hotel walked up and asked if he could help me. In gasping breaths, I explained the situation.

He told me to relax, and called immediately to the front desk to see if it had been turned in. No luck.

With him in the lead, we commenced a rescue search for my beloved bag. He searched the conference room again, the lobby, the stairwell, and even called each staff member to see if they had picked it up, not knowing whom it belonged to.

All our efforts were futile.

As I sat, ready to have a panic attack, he asked the one question I needed, "Is there anything I can get you? A drink, maybe?"

I had to be honest, I didn't think my hand was steady enough to hold a drink without spilling it on my suit and making my day even worse.

"You know, I would kill for a cigarette right now."

He immediately walked over to the front desk, asked an employee, and handed me a pack of cigarettes and a lighter.

Although we never found my bag—and have no idea where it went—the fact that he was willing to search with me was a relief.

Broke the Rules for Me
Tanya Donnelly

"The aim of marketing is to know and understand the customer so well the product or service fits him and sells itself."

Peter Drucker

I'm not sure what possessed me to agree to it, but I found myself as the proud new owner of a 28-foot powerboat. Well...at least my husband owned one. He got the fun in the sun, enjoying his high-speed runs, I enjoyed sitting down and paying the bill every month. It was a once in a lifetime opportunity!

Living in Missouri, our choice of lakes is limited the Lake of the Ozarks. Having an uncle that lives there, he got us in contact with a local marina.

From the very outset, it was inherently evident that each employee at the marina took great care in making sure we were not only welcomed, but enjoyed each visit we had there. Even though we didn't buy a boat slip from them, the harbormaster, Eric, agreed to allow us to store the boat in their lot, on their trailer, and would pull it into and out of the water for us each time we came down for the weekend!

When we were talking to him about a problem we were having with the boat, the owner of the marina walked up and asked us about our satisfaction with everything. I replied we were extremely grateful, especially with them taking care of our boat for us. Eric excused us and took me over to the boat. As we walked, he explained that it was the marina's policy not to pull boats in and out for owners who didn't buy a slip. As I began to apologize and offer to take it off their hands, Eric stopped me.

"I never said I was going to stop, I was just informing you on our official policy. As long as the owner doesn't know, we won't have a problem."

That was the kind of service I was continually provided with at the marina. In fact, the service was so good that when someone saw an opportunity to serve us better, even if it conflicted with policy, they would do it. Even something that could get them reprimanded. That's how dedicated to service they are!

"It Is My Pleasure"
Michaela Rowland

"Your needs will be met once you can find a way of projecting energy and fulfilling someone else's need."
Stuart Wilde

I find myself going to the post office often. Whether it is mailing letters or buying stamps for my mother, I always seem to be there. I use the self check-out machine that the post office has available simply because everyone always seems to be afraid of it and I can get in and out faster.

I went in one day with my brother to mail one of his books back to school. He had procrastinated so long that it had to be postmarked by that day and even had to have the delivery receipt so we knew it got there. As we walked in, we were almost tackled by the gigantic line for the teller section. Knowing our secret location to mail, we headed around the corner to the electronic system.

Since I frequent the post office so much, I became friends with the personable and outgoing Postmaster General. There were times I was mailing my packages and he would come over to ask if the machine was working right, since it had been messing up earlier. He was just that service-driven.

When my brother and I walked to our secret location, we found a man mailing what had to of been 100 packages. We took our place behind him and prepared for the long haul. After about five minutes, I heard the postmaster's voice as he laughed at one of a customer's jokes in the never-ending line.

As he turned the corner, his face lit up as he saw me, "Hey buddy, I apologize for the huge lines today. How's it going?" I explained how we were just there to mail my brother's package.

After talking to us for another two or three minutes, he reached for the package and told me, "You just want me to take care of this for you?" I told him about how I had to have it postmarked by today and needed the delivery receipt. He told me it was no problem—his pleasure even—and would take care of it right now in the back.

I started to pull out my credit card, and I told him it was all that I had to pay with. He pushed my hand away and replied, "You catch me when you come in another time and see me." I thanked him again and we left.

The next day we received the delivery confirmation in the mail from the post office. Everything was returned on time because of our overly helpful postmaster. He builds relationships, especially with customers he sees frequently.

Fill a Void
Anonymous

"Every great business is built on friendship."
                                        J.C. Penney

My 86-year-old father passed away about four years ago. As I was in the process of clearing up all of his old business I ended up at his old bank.

When I walked in, the receptionist asked me if there was anything she could help me with. Explaining I was there to close out my father's account, she replied—without me ever stepping foot in the bank before—"Are you Al Holmburger's daughter?"

I was shocked, to say the least.

I replied I was and soon learned that my father used to go into the bank and have coffee with the receptionist at least once a week. While he was taking care of my mother who was struggling with Alzheimer's, my father had a complete social circle outside of our family, all of whom were in the service industry.

It was the butcher down the street, the cashier at Wal-Mart and the receptionist at the bank.

She told me about how my father would sit down, she'd offer him a cup of coffee, and he would stay and visit with her upwards of an hour.

Although he mentioned in passing that my mother was ill, he never discussed it in detail.

She explained, "It started to occur to me that even if I was busy, he would go back out to his truck. Then we would come back in under the guise that he had forgotten something when he knew I was available."

It was an epiphany moment for me to realize that people in the service industry are filling a gap or void for people who are lonely or don't have a complete support system. Instead of my father coming to me, he went to the receptionist and allowed her to help him forget about his trials and tribulations that were at home.

This woman, someone I'd never seen in my life before, became such an important part of his support system that when I walked in the door she didn't need to question who I was. She knew I was Al's daughter. And that is great service.

Notes

1.) How can you become an important part of a customer's life?

_____

_____

_____

_____

_____

2.) How do you fulfill others' needs?

_____

_____

_____

_____

3.) When is the last time you broke a rule to help a customer?

_____

_____

_____

_____

Characteristics of the Best Service

Gave the little extra
Personalized
Took extra time
Trusted
Filled a void
Knew wants
Fixed Mistakes
Exceeded Expectations
Treated like Royalty
Served the unknown
Took Ownership
Better than competition
Made life easier
Fit budgets
Protected assets
Listened
Flattered
Didn't push products
Went a step farther
Helped in crisis
Cut red tape
Made wishes come true
Adapted to needs
Focused on problem

Never gave excuses
Created happiness
Provided assistance
Used common sense
Different
Diffused stress
Sound advice
Became a tradition
Never pressured
Became a benchmark
Personal concern
Knew names
Supported
Customer Drive
Friendly
Outgoing
Welcoming
Positive
Attention to detail
Encouraging
Humorous
Optimistic
Gave confidence
Approachable

My Own 21 Lessons of Best Service

_____

_____

_____

_____

_____

_____

_____

_____

_____

_____

_____

_____

_____

_____

_____

_____

_____

_____

_____

_____

_____

_____

_____

_____

About the Authors

Quentin Templeton currently a student at Northwest Missouri State University in Maryville, Missouri. Majoring in Business Management and Spanish, Quentin plans to graduate in the spring of 2011. Active in several student organizations and Residential Life, Quentin plans to attend law school after graduating.

Quentin is an Eagle Scout and has been trained at the regional and national level in youth leadership development. He is also an avid scuba diver.

Quentin lives in Kearney, Missouri.

Mark Arnold, CCUE, is an acclaimed speaker, brand expert and strategic planner. Mark speaks regularly to audiences around the country on branding, marketing, strategy, leadership, personal growth and generational issues. With over 20 years experience in the financial services industry, Mark's breadth of knowledge covers areas such as marketing, business development, human resources, training, and sales.

He is also president of On the Mark Strategies, a consulting firm specializing in branding and strategic planning. Not a mere consultant, Mark helps "mark organizations for success" by partnering with them to help achieve their desired strategic goals. Some of the services Mark provides include strategic planning, brand planning, leadership/management training, marketing planning and staff training. Mark is the author of multiple books, including *Think Huge: Elevating Your Life and Your Business*, *My Best Service Ever* and *Marketing Across the Generations: Gen. X.*

Rory Rowland is the president and founder of Rowland Consulting. Rory helps organizations get the best results, and helps managers and leaders earn the trust, respect and admiration of their employees. Rory helps organizations with strategic planning, service selling training, and change management across the nation.

Rory is the former president of two financial institutions. He holds a Bachelor in Economics from the University of Central Missouri, an MBA from the University of Missouri, Kansas City. Rory's previous book is *My Best Boss Ever: How the best bosses get the best results and earn the trust, respect and admiration of their employees.*

Quick Order Form

Web: www.markarnold.com

Telephone: 214-538-4147

Email: mark@markarnold.com

Mail: Mark Arnold
1709 Flowers Drive
Carrollton, TX 75007

Please send me copies of "Think Huge" $19.95 each and $3.99 for shipping and handling. Please call for quantity discounts. I understand that these orders come with a lifetime guarantee. If I'm not happy, Mark's not happy.

_____

_____

_____

Please send me FREE information on:

☐ Books   ☐ Speaking   ☐ Consulting

Name: _____

Address: _____

City: _____ State: _____ Zip:_____

Telephone: _____

Email Address: _____

143

Quick Order Form

Web: www.markarnold.com

Telephone: 214-538-4147

Email: mark@markarnold.com

Mail: Mark Arnold
                  1709 Flowers Drive
                  Carrollton, TX 75007

Please send me copies of "Think Huge" $19.95 each and $3.99 for shipping and handling. Please call for quantity discounts. I understand that these orders come with a lifetime guarantee. If I'm not happy, Mark's not happy.

_____

_____

_____

Please send me FREE information on:

☐ Books   ☐ Speaking   ☐ Consulting

Name: _____

Address: _____

City: _____ State: _____ Zip:_____

Telephone: _____

Email Address: _____

Quick Order Form

Web: www.markarnold.com

Telephone: 214-538-4147

Email: mark@markarnold.com

Mail: Mark Arnold
                  1709 Flowers Drive
                  Carrollton, TX 75007

Please send me copies of "Think Huge" $19.95 each and $3.99 for shipping and handling. Please call for quantity discounts. I understand that these orders come with a lifetime guarantee. If I'm not happy, Mark's not happy.

_____

_____

_____

Please send me FREE information on:

☐ Books   ☐ Speaking   ☐ Consulting

Name: _____

Address: _____

City: _____ State: _____ Zip: _____

Telephone: _____

Email Address: _____

My Best Service Ever